A Treasury of
Illustrations and Quotations
from *Walking With Jesus*

A Treasury of Illustrations and Quotations from *Walking With Jesus*

WALKING WITH JESUS
VOLUME NINE

*An Expository Commentary
Based upon Paul's Letter
to the Ephesians*

ROBERT B. CALLAHAN, SR.

FOREWORD BY
MATTHEW MCCOLLUM

PREFACE BY
JEFF INGRAM

RESOURCE *Publications* • Eugene, Oregon

A TREASURY OF ILLUSTRATIONS AND QUOTATIONS FROM
WALKING WITH JESUS
An Expository Commentary Based upon Paul's Letter to the Ephesians

Copyright © 2015 Robert B. Callahan. All rights reserved. Except for brief quotations in critical publications or reviews, no part of this book may be reproduced in any manner without prior written permission from the publisher. Write: Permissions. Wipf and Stock Publishers, 199 W. 8th Ave., Suite 3, Eugene, OR 97401.

Resource Publications
An Imprint of Wipf and Stock Publishers
199 W. 8th Ave., Suite 3
Eugene, OR 97401

www.wipfandstock.com

ISBN 13: 978-1-60899-653-7

Manufactured in the U.S.A.   06/01/2015

For my wife, Ginger,
whose encouragement, faith,
love, and objectivity contributed
significantly to *Walking With Jesus*

Ephesians "brings one into an atmosphere of unbounded spiritual affluence that creates within one's heart deepest peace and assurance. It is impossible to live habitually in Ephesians and be depressed."

—Ruth Paxson

Contents

Foreword by Matthew McCollum   xi
Preface by Jeff Ingram   ix
Acknowledgments   xiii
Introduction   xv

1	Atonement	1
2	Baptism	3
3	Blasphemy	5
4	Christ Jesus	6
5	Christlike Conduct	19
6	Christ's Teachings	35
7	Discipleship	39
8	Faith	47
9	Forgiveness	61
10	God the Father	63
11	God's Children	69
12	God's Love	78
13	God's Power	84
14	God's Providence	88
15	God's Truth	90
16	Grace	93
17	Holiness	98
18	Holy Communion	100
19	Holy Spirit	102
20	Humility	111

21	Kingdom of God	112
22	Marriage	113
23	Mercy	117
24	Obedience	119
25	Prayer	122
26	Preaching / Teaching	129
27	Redemption / Salvation	139
28	Revelation	148
29	Righteousness	150
30	Sanctification	155
31	Satan / Devil	160
32	Self	168
33	Sin / Sinner	173
34	The Church	180
35	Wisdom	184
36	Word of God	185
37	Wrath of God	196

Preface

Robert Callahan's work, *A Treasury of Quotations and Illustrations*, is a treasure for anyone who prepares sermons, lessons, or devotionals. It is apparent Bob has put into this work untold hours of work and study as he has in his previous volumes on Ephesians. Drawing from such great theologians as John Calvin, William Gurnall, Markus Barth, Martyn Lloyd-Jones, and others, this collection provides pastors and teachers a valuable resource to provide richness and fullness to any message. It is obvious Mr. Callahan is passionate about our Lord and the Apostle Paul's letter to the Ephesians.

Reverend Jeff Ingram

Foreword

If preaching and teaching the gospel is a high calling in your life, this resource can be incredibly valuable. For anyone who opens the Word of God for the people of God, this book features hundreds of illustrations, quotes, and real-life stories to help the listener connect the dots. This collection is not meant to take away from the discipline of research and study. Its purpose is to augment it. The preacher or teacher should always be about the hard work of exegesis, word study, prayer, and analysis of the text. This volume doesn't replace that necessary work, it lays along-side those other tools. Each illustration can deepen the reader's or hearer's understanding of the text for the sole purpose of glorifying God and encouraging the saints.

Robert Callahan has devoted much of his life to the accurate, practical teaching and application of God's Word. He is a gifted writer and he is committed to the life of the church. These quotes are taken from his eight volume commentary based on Paul's letter to the Ephesians. The illustrations have been grouped by subject matter and then alphabetized for quick and easy access. All the major theological themes such as the Trinity, the Holy Spirit, suffering and evil, the church, and the person and work of Jesus Christ are covered. In addition to quotes from Robert Callahan, there are illustrations from other voices both modern and historical—John Calvin, John Leith, Martyn Lloyd-Jones, Ruth Paxson, William Gurnall, and many, many others.

Whether you are putting the finishing touches on Sunday's sermon or you're trying to draw out the implications of a particular doctrine that you're teaching, this is a helpful tool to bring the gospel to life. This collection of serious, thought-provoking, and heart-warming material is a gold-mine for teachers and preachers. It's part of a process that can transform both the listener and the speaker.

Reverend Matthew McCollum

Acknowledgments

The crafting of *Walking With Jesus* was not a "one man show" but numerous people working together to present a formidable work. Three guiding lights have been paramount in the minds of those making significant contributions: one, presenting the theology in accord with the tenets of the Reformed Faith; two, employing language that presents the Gospel in a meaningful and understandable light; and, three, expounding upon Scripture in a clear, concise, and forthright manner. It has been God's blessing that the following ministers have enthusiastically and willingly provided their time and talents to enhance this work. They are:

> Reverend Jeff Ingram, Associate Pastor, First Baptist Church, Fairhope, AL
>
> Reverend Matthew McCollum, Pastor, Trinity Presbyterian Church, Fairhope, AL
>
> Wick Skinner made invaluable contributions through his attention to details, grammar, and vocabulary.

Without the knowledge, wisdom, and encouragement of these individuals this work would neither have become a reality nor available to individuals seeking a better understanding of the teachings of the Scripture and the joy of walking daily with the Lord Jesus.

It is not possible to thank them sufficiently for their dedication to making this volume a desirable repository of Christian truths, and in so doing to cheerfully work on draft after draft, to recommend enhancements, and to make appropriate changes in the text. Their unselfish contributions are too many to enumerate. May God bless them.

Introduction

A Treasury of Quotations and Illustrations is an afterthought and by-product of editing the eight volumes of the *Walking With Jesus Commentary on Paul's Epistle to the Ephesians*. Midway through the process it became evident that there were a number of significant statements and illustrations to compile and share with others.

Therefore, the process began to accumulate appropriate expressions and illustrations regarding the Triune God, the Christian faith, and the challenges facing individuals committed to following Christ in their daily walk. This led to establishing subject matter classifications for the material, instead of listing everything by author. This makes it easier and more efficient for the reader. During this process, there was a continuing effort to add appropriate statements and cull those that did not merit further consideration.

The classifications in this Treasury begin with Atonement and Baptism, include among others, Christ Jesus, God, the Father, Discipleship, Faith, Grace, Preaching/Teaching, Satan/Devil, and concludes with the Word of God and the Wrath of God. The primary contributors are St. Augustine, John Calvin, William Gurnall, Martyn Lloyd Lloyd-Jones, Markus Barth and a newcomer to many, Ruth Paxson. Their clarity, faith, insight, understanding, and wisdom are something to behold. They knew their Redeemer and like the apostles they did not hesitate to proclaim the whole Gospel of Christ. They are truly God pleasers, not men pleasers.

Hopefully, this compendium will be a valuable asset to you, the reader, as you search for meaningful quotations and illustrations. May the individual items not only satisfy your interest and needs, but may they stimulate you to: explore other subjects; expound upon the tenets of the Christian faith; present the Lord Jesus Christ as our friend, Lord and Savior.

Robert B. Callahan, Sr.

1

ATONEMENT

For as He (Christ) fastened to the Cross our curse, our sins and also the punishment due to us, so also that bondage of the law and everything that tends to bind consciences. **(John Calvin)**

Christ's will was to do the will of the Father. He was never discouraged from doing His Father's will, even when He went to Calvary's Hill. That was the climax, or pinnacle, of obeying the Father. **(Robert B. Callahan, Sr.)**

A person cannot "Really begin to understand the love of God and the love of the Lord Jesus Christ who does not believe the substitutionary and penal doctrine of the atonement." **(Martyn Lloyd-Jones)**

Nothing ever discouraged our Lord on His way to Jerusalem. He never hurried through certain villages where He was persecuted, or lingered in others where He was blessed. Neither gratitude nor ingratitude turned our Lord one hair's breadth away from His purpose to go up to Jerusalem. **(Oswald Chambers)**

It is the fact that Christ was crucified for me, as He was for the world, that results in my debt being paid, my being pardoned, and my receiving eternal life. **(Robert B. Callahan, Sr.)**

God's gift of His Son was an exercise of divine will and was made for one reason only, to express His love toward us. **(Robert B. Callahan, Sr.)**

Paul and Peter remind us that God's justice and righteousness demanded it, His wrath against sin required it, and His love for us dictated it. **(Robert B. Callahan, Sr.)**

The Atonement of Christ cultivates within the unrighteous person a righteous heart. The remission of sins is tied inextricably to repentance. **(Robert B. Callahan, Sr.)**

The grace of God makes us clean and whole in His sight through the atoning blood of our Lord Jesus Christ. Does that mean there is nothing else for us to do? With respect to our salvation the answer is *Yes*. With respect to our sanctification the answer is *No*. **(Robert B. Callahan, Sr.)**

It is rather fitting that a person cannot really begin to understand the love of God and the love of the Lord Jesus Christ who does not believe the substitutionary and penal Doctrine of Atonement. **(Martyn Lloyd-Jones)**

1 John 1:7 teaches that the bond of our union with God is the blood of Jesus Christ and from this comes the fruit by which our sins are forgiven and we are cleansed. **(Robert B. Callahan, Sr.)**

2

BAPTISM

We do not become Christ's inheritance because we are baptized; however, we are baptized because we are Christ's inheritance. (**Robert B. Callahan, Sr.**)

We need to beware of making baptism essential to salvation. Baptismal regeneration is not taught in scripture. It was introduced in order to establish the power of the priesthood and of the church. (**Robert B. Callahan, Sr.**)

There is an interesting fact here. We have faith only as we receive it. And we have baptism only as we receive it. Faith and baptism belong together. However, baptism does not result from faith and faith does not result from baptism. (**Robert B. Callahan, Sr.**)

Baptism, is not an expression of our faith in God or our love to Him; it is the expression of a Divine thought, it is the symbol of a Divine act. (**R.W. Dale**)

The Apostle by saying, *one baptism* does not mean a rite or something magical. He means there is only one Lord. The one Lord has redeemed us. He has incorporated us into His body. We are to follow His leadership and to subordinate our wills to His will. He is to be our life, and therefore we can say with Paul, *I live, yet not I, but Christ liveth in me.* The old self disappears, the new self is in Christ. (**Robert B. Callahan, Sr.**)

It should be pointed out that the person being baptized accepts the act passively whether an infant, child, or adult. This is important. We do not make ourselves members of the community, we are made members of it! **(Robert B. Callahan, Sr.)**

The connecting factor is the Holy Spirit and the knowledge of faith. This faith confirms itself in baptism. It can be the faith of the community, or of the person performing the act, or the person being baptized. Faith comes first. **(Robert B. Callahan, Sr.)**

Paul, in Romans, describes one of the impacts of being baptized. The person is submersed into the death of Christ and then receives newness of life. When considering this, remember that baptism is an act of separation, of setting aside; it results in being integrated into the community of believers and into a new reality. **(Robert B. Callahan, Sr.)**

Baptism is a figure, . . . of what the Lord Jesus Christ does for us in the process of sanctification. **(Martyn Lloyd-Jones)**

Baptism has a special character. Of course, people want to give it limits or precise definitions, or interpretations. Fixing limits on baptism would be appropriate only if it were the means to an end and that was the only way to attain it; but, then it would not be empowered by the Spirit and designated as a means for receiving the Spirit. It would become something placed in man's hands requiring a specific order and process with the attendant prerequisites and effects. It would become a thing. It would possibly deteriorate into something subject to manipulation and thereby lose the freedom of God moving over and through us by the Holy Spirit. **(Robert B. Callahan, Sr.)**

By virtue of baptism I am destined to become a member of the community, to be integrated into the building, and to renounce my isolation or separation, and to turn to the one who is Lord. We are baptized in the name of the Lord Jesus Christ. **(Robert B. Callahan, Sr.)**

3

BLASPHEMY

The Pharisees and Scribes were distorting the Law and the Ten Commandments. Further, children who were adults were not discharging their responsibility to honor their parents. They were saying that they had dedicated their time and money to the Lord, therefore, they could not care or provide for their parents.

> Jesus said to the Scribes and Pharisees: "*For God commanded, saying, Honor thy father and mother: and He that curseth father or mother, let him die the death. But ye say, Whosoever shall say to his father or his mother, It is a gift, by whatsoever thou mightest be profited by me; And honor not his father or his mother, he shall be free. Thus have ye made the commandment of God of none effect by your tradition.*" [**Matt. 15:4–6**]

Unfortunately, it is those in authority in the church who can distort the teachings of God and thereby mislead those who would follow. (**Robert B. Callahan, Sr.**)

To tell people that what a man believes does not matter as long as he lives a good life and does good is not only denial of the Gospel, it is bound to discourage people from the only truth which can save them. (**Martyn Lloyd-Jones**)

4

CHRIST JESUS

"My Hope Is Built on Nothing Less"
My hope is built on nothing less,
Than Jesus' blood and Righteousness;
I dare not trust the sweetest frame
But wholly lean on Jesus name.
On Christ the Solid Rock I stand;
All other ground is sinking sand.
All other ground is sinking sand.
(Edward Mote)

That his (Paul's) teaching of Christ was not changeable or ambiguous, so as to present Christ in different shapes at different times . . . others, to please men, present Christ under different false disguises, and others again teach a thing one day and the next retract it, out of fear. Such was not Paul's Christ nor the Christ of any apostle . . . For the only true Christ is He in whom can be seen this invariable and perpetual 'yea' which Paul here declares to be characteristic of Him. **(John Calvin)**

There is a gulf between us and God that is revealed in the law. There is only one way it can be bridged. The law can be fulfilled only through the grace that is in and through Jesus Christ. Also, the reality of the image of God is revealed through Him. Jesus is the man for God, out of God, and before God. It is in the Lord Jesus Christ that our rejection is terminated in, through and upon Him. In this manner our judgment is set aside by

God's grace. A peculiarity of this is that only in and through Him does our real rejection come to light. These things cannot be recognized outside the reality of Jesus Christ and Him crucified. **(Robert B. Callahan, Sr.)**

There is no ultimate knowledge of God apart from the Lord Jesus Christ and the full and the perfect revelation that is in Him. **(Martyn Lloyd-Jones)**

Everyone who knows and is persuaded that he is chastised by God ought at once to advance to this realization that it happens because he is loved by God. **(John Calvin)**

The Lord Jesus Christ came to fulfill the law, carry our burdens, redeem us, enlighten us, and discipline us. **(Robert B. Callahan, Sr.)**

When believers find God in the midst of their punishments, they have a sure pledge of His loving kindness. **(John Calvin)**

The difference between the person *in Christ* and the one outside Christ is that the non-Christian's mind is controlled by the world, whereas the person *in Christ* has a mind trans- formed and renewed by the Holy Spirit and therefore controlled by Him. The consequence of being renewed and transformed is that a person thinks in a spiritual manner, or in the Spirit of God. **(Robert B. Callahan, Sr.)**

The reason for strengthening the inner man is the greatness of what is offered and the possibilities for us: that Christ may dwell within our hearts by faith; that we may know the love of God; and that we may be filled with all the fullness of God. These possibilities require being strengthened in order to receive them and deal with the ordeals and temptations of life. **(Robert B. Callahan, Sr.)**

We must learn from the whole of life, because the truly wise man is the one who knows how far short he comes of any complete understanding. **(John Calvin)**

Intellectual lethargy is probably the greatest sin of many members of the community of believers today. Too many are content to recount their early experiences with their primary level of learning, or to base everything on their carnal knowledge. They remain where they began. They do not come to know the unsearchable riches of God's holy truth. Therefore, Paul prays that their minds may be strengthened in order that they may realize the great possibilities of the life *in Christ* and rejoice in them. Then, to bear witness and testimony to the glory of God. (**Robert B. Callahan, Sr.**)

Few have the courage and resolution to grapple with the difficulties that meet them in their way to happiness. (**William Gurnall**)

Christ submitted Himself in a self-denying, self-sacrificing love, even unto death, for His Bride, whom He cherishes and cares for in the most tender manner. The Church, the Bride, responds with the submission of absolute loyalty in yieldedness and obedience. It is the mutual submission of a pure love for a perfect lover. (**Robert B. Callahan, Sr.**)

There are no different or separate ways into the Kingdom of God. There is only one way. There is only one way to have access into the presence of God and that is through the one and only Mediator. The Old Testament figures, the New Testament people, the individuals up to the present time and the ones in the future are all reconciled in and through Christ. There is no other way. This despite the teaching, by some, that many are saved in Christ, by His death and grace and at some future time the Jews will be saved by keeping the law. (**Robert B. Callahan, Sr.**)

He is the presence of power and the radiance of truth in the midst of the world. (**Markus Barth**)

That declares something of God's power and the power of salvation. Either, we become so engrossed in the Cross and our Lord's death, or it becomes so familiar to us that we fail to grasp the sense of power that was involved in Christ's earthly ministry. (**Robert B. Callahan, Sr.**)

Paul stated simply and succinctly that he was not just a prisoner, but a prisoner of Jesus Christ. This was not idle boasting, but a dignified and faithful statement of the facts. The ignominy which some had intended was transferred to the highest glory as Calvin so aptly stated "so highly ought the name of Christ to be revered by us, that what men consider to be the highest reproach, should be to us the greatest honor." **(John Calvin)**

Because first He [Christ] is the eternal wisdom and will of God, and secondly, because He is the express image of His purpose. **(John Calvin)**

The Lord comes to our aid. Many foes are in arms against us, but in God's keeping we are safe. In a word, though we are brought so low that all seems over with us, yet we do not perish. You see how he turned to his own advantage every charge that the wicked (one) brings against him. **(John Calvin)**

He openly declares that He does not pray for the world, for He is solicitous only for His own flock which He received from the Father's hand. Christ expressly declares that they who are given to Him belong to the Father. **(John Calvin)**

Paul praises Christ in such a way that neither death, nor former divisions, nor institutions, nor structures, and certainly not marriage, can escape the power and riches of grace. **(Markus Barth)**

As we conclude our consideration of boldness, access and confidence it is beneficial to examine Calvin's teaching about Christ and our salvation, about doctrine and its application. He says:

- "We see that our whole salvation and all its parts are comprehended in Christ [**Acts 4:12**],
- We should not derive the least potion from anywhere else,
- If we seek salvation, we are taught by the very name of Jesus, that it is 'of him.' [**1 Cor. 1:30**]
- If we seek strength, it is in His dominion,
- If purity, in his conception,
- If gentleness, in His birth, [**Heb. 2:17**]
- If we seek redemption, it is in His passion,
- If acquittal, in His condemnation,
- If remission of the curse, in His Cross [**Gal. 3:13**]

- If satisfaction, in His sacrifice,
- If purification, in His blood,
- If reconciliation, in His descent into hell,
- If mortification of the flesh, in His tomb,
- If newness of life, in His resurrection,
- If immortality, in the same,
- If inheritance of the Heavenly Kingdom, in His entrance into Heaven,
- If protection, security, and an abundant supply of blessings, in His Kingdom,
- If untroubled expectation of judgment, in the power given to Him to judge."

(John Calvin)

We are to know how to be strengthened, how to prepare our hearts, and how to be rooted and grounded in love. Paul "explains the nature of the strength of the inward man." God placed the fullness of all gifts in Christ, so the person who has been strengthened with might by the Spirit and has Christ dwelling in his or her heart can want for nothing. **(John Calvin)**

What is to be preached and taught? First, the Gospel is Christ Himself. He is the *unsearchable riches,* He is the message of Christianity and its Gospel, everything is in Him and nothing is apart from Him. To have anything, we must have contact with Him and be in Him. We are united to Him and we are to draw from Him. Though what He gives is of vast importance, it takes second place to what and who He is. **(Robert B. Callahan, Sr.)**

The sense is that some (of the disciples) hesitated at first until Christ approached them nearer and more intimately. When they knew him in truth and certainty, then they worshipped Him. There is no doubt that his approach to them took away all doubts. Before relating that the office of teaching was laid upon them, Matthew says that Christ spoke first of His power, and rightly so . . . . The Apostles would never be persuaded to undertake such a task of difficulty unless they knew that their Champion sat in heaven, and that supreme power was given to him. **(John Calvin)**

It is one thing to accept the fact that, yes, the Lord Jesus Christ loves the church, that He nourishes and cherishes Her. But, it is entirely different to accept the fact that the Lord Jesus Christ loves me, that He nourishes and cherishes me—with all my warts, blemishes, spots, stains, and wrinkles. **(Robert B. Callahan, Sr.)**

And can it be, that I should gain an interest in the Saviour's blood? Died He for me, who caused His Pain? For me, who Him to death pursued? Amazing love! How can it be, that thou, my God, should die for me? **(Charles Wesley)**

Jesus Christ as attested to us in Holy Scripture is the one Word of God whom we must hear and whom we must trust and obey in life and in death. **(The Barmen Declaration)**

It is Christ who has triumphed, not us. But as members of His body we are victorious. Have you ever noticed how people like to be part of the winning team or party? Paul knew he was part of the winning team. He knew the Captain. He mentions the Lord Jesus no less than sixty-six times in this letter to the Ephesians. **(Robert B. Callahan, Sr.)**

Lord Jesus, make thyself to me, a living bright reality; more present to faith's vision, more keen than any outward object seen; more dear, more intimately nigh than e'en the sweetest earthly tie. **(Hudson Taylor)**

Nothing ever discouraged our Lord on His way to Jerusalem. He never hurried through certain villages where He was persecuted or lingered in others where He was blessed. Neither gratitude nor ingratitude turned our Lord one hair's breadth away from His Father's purpose for Him to go up to Jerusalem. **(Oswald Chambers)**

There needs to be an awakening of our minds to the presence of Christ, to the reality of being members of His body, to confessing our sins, to the need for forgiveness, and to accepting with humility and confidence His forgiveness of our sins. **(Robert B. Callahan, Sr.)**

"Fight the Good Fight"

Fight the good fight with all thy might;
Christ is thy strength, and Christ thy right;
Lay hold on life, and it shall be
Thy joy and crown eternally.

Run the straight race through God's good grace,
Lift up thine eyes, and seek His face;
Life with its way before thee lies;
Christ is the way, and Christ the prize.

Cast care aside; lean on thy guide,
Lean and His mercy will provide;
Lean and the trusting soul shall prove
Christ is its life, and Christ its love.

Faint not nor fear, His arm is near;
He changeth not, and thou art dear;
Only believe, and thou shalt see,
That Christ is all in all to thee.
(John S.B. Monsell)

God's gift of His son was an exercise of divine will and was made for one reason only, to express His love toward us. (**Robert B. Callahan, Sr.**)

Since in Christ we are a fruitful vine, out of Christ what are we but withered little branches. (**St. Augustine**)

There needs to be an awaking of our minds to the presence of Christ, to the reality of being members of His body, to recognizing our sins and the need for forgiveness, and to accepting with humility and confidence His forgiveness of our sins. (**Robert B. Callahan, Sr.**)

There is a distinct difference between believing in Christ and having Christ dwell in your heart and mind. To believe in the Lord Jesus Christ is not the end of Christianity. On the contrary, it is only the beginning. It is absolutely essential to believe the truth about His person and His work. (**Robert B. Callahan, Sr.**)

A poem by John Ryland, a preacher in the late 1700's and early 1800's, expresses these thoughts fully:

"O Lord I Would Delight in Thee"

O Lord, I would delight in Thee
And on Thy care depend;
To thee in every trouble flee,
My best, my only friend.

When all created streams are dried
Thy fullness is the same;
May I with this be satisfied
And glory in Thy Name!

No good in creatures can be found
But may be found in Thee;
I must have all things and abound,
While God is God to me.

He that has made my heaven secure
Will here all good provide;
While Christ is rich, can I be poor?
What can I ask beside?

O Lord, I cast my care on Thee;
I triumph and adore,
Henceforth my great concern shall be
To love and please Thee more.
(John Ryland)

We are to see Christ as the Messiah, as the One who redeems us, who illuminates our way, who lightens our load, who removes blindness and hardness from our hearts, and as the One who walks with us, if we let Him and will share with Him. **(Robert B. Callahan, Sr.)**

The life in Christ requires obedience to God's commandments, the Sermon on the Mount, the New Testament epistles, and the Ten Commandments. **(Robert B. Callahan, Sr.)**

Suppose there is a well of fathomless trouble inside your heart, and Jesus comes and says, "Let not your heart be troubled": and you shrug your shoulders and say, "But, Lord the well is deep; you cannot draw up quietness and comfort out of it." No, He will bring them down from above. Jesus does not bring anything up from the wells of human nature. (**Oswald Chambers**)

Who was the greatest meddler of all time? There is no question that it was, is, and will be the Lord Jesus Christ. (**Robert B. Callahan, Sr.**)

Ernest Logan, an Irishman who was an associate minister, at the First Presbyterian Church in Pittsburgh would ask individuals joining the Church about their Christian experiences. He would listen patiently as they talked about their lives as children and growing up in a fine home, about the various jobs or functions they had performed in the churches to which they had belonged, or about the boards on which they may have served.

Then he would say, "Aye that is all very well and good, but would ye mind telling me about your relationship with the Lord Jesus Christ?" Usually, this would cause consternation and long pauses before responding. Ernest had a way of cutting to the heart of the matter. It is our relationship with Christ that is important, nothing more, nothing less, nothing else. (**Robert B. Callahan, Sr.**)

Christ's will was to do the will of the Father. He was never discouraged from doing His Father's will, even when He went to Calvary's Hill. That was the pinnacle of obeying the Father. (**Robert B. Callahan, Sr.**)

It is not Christ *for* me unless I am determined to have Christ formed *in* me. (**Oswald Chambers**)

Many people think the day of giving an account will never come, that it will pass them by. These people should remember the day of the Crucifixion: when Christ was scourged, when He climbed Calvary's Hill, when He was crucified, when He shed His blood and died. We are to remember that day. But, thank God the third day came when He rose from the dead. Yes, the day of giving an account will come! (**Robert B. Callahan, Sr.**)

Life without Christ is always empty; it is always vain; it takes from you; and it takes out of you. It leaves you an empty husk with nothing to offer. (**Robert B. Callahan, Sr.**)

> Twixt gleams of joy and clouds of doubt
> Our feelings come and go;
> Our best estate is tossed about
> In ceaseless ebb and flow:
> No mood of feeling, form of thought,
> Is constant for a day;
> But thou, O Lord, thou changest not,
> The same thou art always.
> I grasp thy strength, make it mine own,
> My heart with peace is blest;
> I lose my hold, and then comes down
> Darkness and cold unrest.
> Let me no more my comfort drown
> From my frail hold of thee;
> In this alone rejoice with awe –
> Thy mighty grasp of me. *
> (**Author Unknown**)

The title Son of God contains additional thoughts and concepts, notably that Jesus is the servant of God and also in God's eternity. This is seen in the preexistence of Jesus; the One who has come out of God's eternity, not just out of time; the only begotten Son of God; and God's resounding statement, *This my beloved Son.* (**Robert B. Callahan, Sr.**)

It should be noted as Otto Weber says that "whoever speaks of Kyrios is speaking of God, of God as revealed in His Lordship" or in His Son. The question of Christ's deity and its implications of His lordship over the world are to be considered in the New Testament framework; primarily in connection with His work rather than His being.

Second, we are to consider the Lord Jesus Christ as our Master. The Master yesterday, today and tomorrow. The term "kyrios" means the present Lord and that the community is not addressing or calling upon someone who had been in the past. **(Otto Weber)**

The doctrine of the two natures in one person. The two natures are so joined together that they cannot be separated. Christ as God, Christ as man. Possibly it is better stated as God in man or in the form of man. It is not a case of Christ as God or Christ as man and the one is isolated or separated from the other. That is not to be done. Christ is always God-man.

We are not to say that He did or does certain things as God and other things as man. Christ is always indivisible and He cannot be divided. He is One, He has always been One and He always will be One. **(Robert B. Callahan, Sr.)**

Paul well defines those who are endowed with the spiritual power of God as those in whom Christ dwells. **(John Calvin)**

A divinely determined diversity in the divinely purposed unity in the Body of Christ. **(Ruth Paxson)**

What does Christ want? "He wants us to desire nothing more than the light." **(John Calvin)**

The doctrine of justification describes God's reconciling work in Jesus Christ as the act through which man, in himself unrighteous, is truly brought into harmony with God, and not just in name only. **(Otto Weber)**

He (the Apostle John) states he is teaching what he thoroughly learned from the Master. His teachings are not based upon rumors, nor does he present them thoughtlessly. He says a person cannot be a fit teacher who has not first been a student of Jesus', learned from Him, and accepted the authority of His teachings. Oh, that teachers and preachers would follow in his footsteps. **(Robert B. Callahan, Sr.)**

To put on Christ means . . . to be defended on every side by the power of His Spirit, and thus rendered fit to discharge all the duties of holiness.
(Robert B. Callahan, Sr.)

The greatest triumph, which God ever won, was when Christ, after subduing sin, conquering death, and putting Satan to flight rose majestically to heaven, that He might exercise His glorious reign over the church.
(John Calvin)

"Jesus, the Very Thought of Thee"

Jesus the very thought of thee,
With sweetness fills the breast.

O hope of every contrite heart,
O joy of all the meek,

To those who fall how kind thou art,
How good to those who seek!

But what to those who find?
Ah, this Nor tongue nor pen can show;

The love of Jesus, what it is,
None but His loved ones know.
(Bernard of Clairvaux)

O Jesus, King most wonderful,
Thou conqueror renowned,
Thou sweetness most ineffable
In whom all joys are found.

When once thou visitest the heart
Then truth begins to shine;
Then earthly vanities depart;
Then kindles love divine.
(Bernard of Clairvaux)

The reason the Lord Jesus came into the world. There was no other way! Nothing else would do. There had to be the incarnation, the road to Calvary's Hill, the Crucifixion, the shedding of Christ's blood, and the

Resurrection. Why? Because, it was necessary for Christ to come, to seek, and to save the lost. There was no other way. **(Robert B. Callahan, Sr.)**

The Lord Jesus Christ came to: fulfill the law, carry our burdens, redeem us, enlighten us, and discipline us. **(Robert B. Callahan, Sr.)**

Dr. Robert Ferguson at the conclusion of a sermon on the Twenty-third Psalm told about a number of people attending a party, one of whom was a renowned actor. After dinner the conversation turned to religion. One of the guests asked the actor to recite the Twenty-third Psalm. He recited it beautifully. When he finished, there were many "ohs" and "ahs" and compliments.

Also, in attendance was an elderly or should we say mature minister. After the congratulatory conversation died down, the actor sincerely asked the minister to say the Twenty-third Psalm. After some encouragement, he did. When he finished saying, *And I will dwell in the house of the Lord forever* there was complete silence, there was a hush over the group that lasted a long, long time. Finally, the actor broke the silence saying, "Pastor, I know the Twenty-third Psalm, but you know the Shepherd." **(Robert B. Callahan, Sr.)**

Christ's will was to do the will of the Father. He was never discouraged from doing His Father's will, not even when He went to Calvary's Hill. **(Robert B. Callahan, Sr.)**

Truth is a pure and right knowledge of God, and Jesus Christ is that Truth providing knowledge of God. **(Robert B. Callahan, Sr.)**

5

CHRISTLIKE CONDUCT

We are to live an orderly and disciplined life. We are not to be erratic and inconsistent. "The Christian is a man who sees life steadily and he sees it whole, and therefore he is not erratic." **(Matthew Arnold)**

If we really love Jesus then we will keep His commandments. People have many opinions about love. This is especially true about the love of Christ. However, true love of Christ is really determined by keeping His teachings and being obedient unto Him. This is the unique rule. However, we should realize that our affections and our emotions can be sinful and our love for Christ can be at fault unless it exhibits and expresses true and pure obedience to Him. Thy will be done! **(Robert B. Callahan, Sr.)**

We cannot show pure obedience unless we know Him, His teachings and the truth that is in Him. **(Robert B. Callahan, Sr.)**

The Apostle Paul, as well as the other New Testament writers, understood the Master's way of teaching, explaining God's law, putting things into practice and growing in the Lord. Paul did not expect instant success or compliance, but he did expect the members of Christ's body to know, to understand, to gain knowledge, to try, to rely upon the power of the Holy Spirit, and to deny themselves. **(Robert B. Callahan, Sr.)**

God has told us we would have temptations, trials, testings, so we must be prepared to stand the strain of the slippery paths of temptation and the stony hills of adversity and affliction . . . as we walk through this disordered world there are a thousand things to bruise and wound us. **(Ruth Paxson)**

We are not to strive to attain the favor of men in such a way that we refuse to incur the hatred of any for the sake of Christ . . . there are, . . . some who, . . . are nonetheless hated even by their nearest relations on account of the Gospel. **(John Calvin)**

Anyone who has the firm conviction that he will never be forsaken by the Lord will not be unduly anxious because he will depend on His providence. **(John Calvin)**

We are to remain connected to the Lord Jesus no matter where we are, what we are doing, or what the conditions may be. We are to stay connected through prayer. **(Georgina Dufoix)**

There is nothing in scripture which may not contribute to your instruction and the training of your life. **(John Calvin)**

The Apostle Paul had the thorn in the flesh, he was opposed, rejected and buffeted. He besought the Lord three times in prayer. What answer did he receive? **(St. Augustine)**

If the Lord aids us by His extraordinary power, we have no reason to be irresolute in battle. **(John Calvin)**

The question is, what is acceptable to the Lord?
- Living according to the teachings of our Lord;
- Living with an understanding of the nature of sin;
- Living with a meaningful knowledge of the Cross, the suffering, the bloodshed for us collectively and individually;
- Living in search of the spiritual food and water;
- Living with the knowledge of God's forgiveness in the Lord Jesus Christ;
- Living by trying to follow in the footsteps of our Lord;

- Living and searching for the will of God; and
- Living a life of faith.

    (Robert B. Callahan, Sr.)

There is a point in our lives in Christ where we must begin to live in the promises we have embraced. **(Robert B. Callahan, Sr.)**

The revelation of Christ in truth must result in the realization of Christ in life. **(Ruth Paxson)**

Paul does not boast in words, but proves that in reality Christ speaks through him. Further, he convinces the Corinthians that they should listen to him and to his claims. When it becomes clear that it is God's Word being proclaimed then what Paul says holds true if people do not believe, then they are disbelieving God. This is true of preachers and teachers. **(Robert B. Callahan, Sr.)**

The purpose, or business, of Christianity is not to improve the world. It is to save people from it. Further, to form a new realm, a new kingdom, and a new humanity. They were to learn Christ so that the powers of the world could not prevail against them. **(Robert B. Callahan, Sr.)**

We are to be new wineskins for the new wine of Jesus every day. We are to be elastic, so that we can expand to hold the richness and fullness of the new wine, we are to be flexible so that the new wine can ferment within us so that we can be used as He would use us, and we are to be adjustable so that we can meet the demands and requirements placed upon us. **(Robert B. Callahan, Sr.)**

No man is born either naturally or supernaturally with character, he has to make character. Nor are we born with habits; we have to form habits on the basis of the new life God has put into us. **(Oswald Chambers)**

Paul realized that he was grasped by Christ in order that he might grasp the Lord Jesus. O' pray God that we might recognize and accept both of these points since they go together. **(Robert B. Callahan, Sr.)**

The New Testament emphasizes one main point that is diametrically opposed to the way most, and I say most, church members think and that is the New Testament does not emphasize what we do, but what we are and what we are to become.

That bears repeating: The New Testament does not emphasize what we do, but what we are and what we are to become. **(Robert B. Callahan, Sr.)**

I do not find the Apostle telling me to hand it over to the Lord and that He will fight my battles for me while I just sit back and enjoy the fruit of His victory. It is not here! I have to fight! **(Martyn Lloyd-Jones)**

Paul says the way to deal with the conditions, or situations, encountered in daily living is to *"be filled with the Spirit."* He says that as members of Christ's body, they are to address things differently, they are to act and react in a different manner. May we reach the point of maturity where we say, *"My goal is God Himself, not joy nor peace, Nor even blessing, but Himself, my God."* **(Robert B. Callahan, Sr.)**

Our Scripture exhorts us to be obedient to the governing authorities. Peter says that we are to do the *"will of God"* and *"put to silence the ignorance of foolish men."* When people are deprived of understanding and reason concerning the will of God and His teachings, then they cannot conduct themselves according to His commands. **(Robert B. Callahan, Sr.)**

Think about Martin Luther. What did he discover?

There he was, a monk. A knowledgeable, intelligent person well versed in the teachings of the church. There he was, fasting, praying, studying, and sweating:

- Wrestling with the spiritual enemies;
- Then, at last, it was revealed unto him by the Holy Spirit;
- Faith in Christ was not separating oneself from the world. It was separating oneself unto Christ;
- Talk about changing the mind-set. Luther did;
- He realized a person could be separated to Christ even though he was in the midst of the world;

- As Luther put it, "you could be a Christian sweeping a floor."

(Robert B. Callahan, Sr.)

Paul tells us what blessings we have received, but also, he wishes to forewarn and to forearm us. He wants to prepare us for the opposition we will encounter. He wants us to know that following Christ is not easy, that all the problems of life will not disappear. The New Testament epistles were written not to tell us how to live a life of ease, but how to withstand the pressures, subtleties, disappointments, defeats, and failures of life and to be *'more than conquerors'* in Christ. **(Robert B. Callahan, Sr.)**

The godly calmly wait for Christ and do not dread His presence. **(John Calvin)**

The Apostle John, by many arguments proves that faith is joined to a holy and pure life. First that we are spiritually begotten in the likeness of Christ. From this it follows that no one is born of Christ save He who lives righteously. **(John Calvin)**

Anyone who ought to grow with time (it) is inexcusable if he remains forever a child. **(John Calvin)**

Please note what Scripture says. It says *"having on,"* it does not say "have a breastplate," rather it says, *"having on."* **(Robert B. Callahan, Sr.)**

A vivid description of how we are to walk (as members of Christ's body) is contained in the following words of the esteemed **Bishop Moule**, "The appeal is again for a grave remembrance that a walk in the light is no mere promenade, smooth and easy, but a march, resolved and full of purpose, cautious against the enemy, watchful for opportunity for the King, and self-controlled in every habit, and possible only in the power of the eternal Spirit."

Paul tells the Colossians that they are to put on the new man as God's elect or chosen ones. Calvin says, "This can be paraphrased to say, God has chosen you to Himself, has sanctified you, and received you unto His love on the condition that you shall be merciful." To this the Apostle adds you shall be kindness, humility, meekness, long-suffering, forbearing, and forgiving. **(John Calvin)**

No greater absurdity, and indeed no greater dishonor or shame than that the spiritual grace of Christ should have less influence over them than earthly freedom. **(John Calvin)**

What Christianity is interested in is the way in which a Christian slave behaves towards his Master, and, how the Master behaves towards his slave. It does not deal directly with the questions of slavery per se. **(Martyn Lloyd-Jones)**

This statement the Kingdom of God does not mean Heaven. It means entering into a relationship with God. As Calvin says, "It is rather a spiritual life, which is begun by faith in this world and daily increases according to the continual progress of faith." What is the meaning of this? No one can be truly gathered into Christ's Body and counted among the children of God until he has been renewed, or reborn. **(John Calvin)**

Sin and righteousness are so opposed to one another that anyone who devotes himself to the one must leave the other. **(John Calvin)**

The word constrain points out that everyone who truly considers and ponders the wonderful love that Christ has shown us in His death, cannot but be bound to Him by the tightest chain so as to devote Himself to His service. **(John Calvin)**

The appeal is again for a grave remembrance that a walk in the light is no mere promenade, smooth and easy, but a march, resolved and full of purpose, cautious against the enemy, watchful for opportunity for the King, and self controlled in every habit, and possible only in the power of the eternal Spirit. **(Bishop Moule)**

He wants true growth for these followers, which Calvin identifies as "progress in knowledge and (in) *understanding* and in love . . . For the more we progress in knowledge, the more ought our love to increase." **(John Calvin)**

We are not to be unwilling to hear Him (Christ) speaking by the tongue of men. **(John Calvin)**

Paul exhorts the Philippians to imitate him, that they may at last reach the same goal, that they may mind the same thing and walk by the same rule. For where sincere affection flourishes, such as reigned in Paul, the way is easy to a holy and godly concord. **(John Calvin)**

The greatest saints have always testified to the fierceness of the battle, to their own weakness, to their own inability. **(Martyn Lloyd-Jones)**

To put on Christ means here to be defended on every side by the power of His Spirit, and thus rendered fit to discharge all the duties of holiness. **(John Calvin)**

My life ought to provide some sort of example to others. Therefore, I take pains to live in such a way that my character and conduct do not conflict with what I teach (or profess), and that I may not, therefore, neglect the very things which I demand of others (or myself) so involving myself in great disgrace and causing serious offence to my brothers (and sisters). **(John Calvin)**

Paul here reminds them, that, while masters rule over their servants, they have the same Master in heaven, to whom they must render an account. **(John Calvin)**

If we want to be kept according to the rule which Christ laid down, we must not desire immunity from evils or pray to God to convey us straightway into blessed rest, but must remain content with the certain assurance of victory and meanwhile resist bravely all the evils from which Christ prayed to His Father that we might have a happy issue. **(John Calvin)**

He is truly humble who neither claims anything for himself over against God, nor proudly despises his brethren, affecting superiority, but regards it sufficient to be reckoned as one of the members of Christ and desires nothing but that the Head (Christ) alone have the pre-eminence. **(John Calvin)**

We make room for Christ's grace when with a resigned mind we feel and confess our own weakness. (**John Calvin**)

When a person truly desires to be strong, he must not also refuse to be weak. (**John Calvin**)

The fruit of the lips reveals the quality of the tree. Bad language and foul talk defile the whole man and manifest his corruption. (**Markus Barth**)

He means by this that there is no place for laziness or for following the calling of God easily or carelessly, but keen zeal is a necessity, as though He were saying, put forth every effort and let everyone see it. (**John Calvin**)

It is a definite sign of our union with God when we are conformed to Him. However, let us make one point clear: it is not the purity of our daily living that reconciles us to God. It is when God's purity shines in us that our unity with Him is assured. Of course, it must be stated and acknowledged that whenever God's holiness fills us there is no room for filth, uncleanness and darkness. We cannot live properly unless we cleave to God. Our fellowship is to be with God, not just with one another. (**Robert B. Callahan, Sr.**)

However, it can be summed up by saying that what proves we are members of Christ's body, "Is that, over and above everything else, our ultimate, our final consideration is our desire to seek and to know, to discover, the will of the Lord, in order that we may please Him. It is this personal relationship to this blessed Person." (**Martyn Lloyd-Jones**)

The armor which is provided for us by God cannot be used except in fellowship and communion with God. Further, every single piece, excellent though it is in itself, will not suffice us, and will not avail us, unless always and at all times we are in a living relationship to God and receiving strength and power from Him. (**Martyn Lloyd-Jones**)

The image of God in holiness and righteousness is reborn in us on the condition of our sharing in eternal life and glory. (**John Calvin**)

I wish you to remember this commandment always, as if it were a law recently made. **(John Calvin)**

It is important to note, . . . that Christ selected people to teach the Gospel who would be faithful witnesses. Those selected were motivated to have fellowship with one another in His name and to receive the blessings available from God through His Son. These factors had a significant impact not only in hearing the Word, but in communicating it. They contributed immeasurably to increasing one's faith and witness, and to applying the Master's teachings. **(Robert B. Callahan, Sr.)**

What God requires is not merely that of action, but also of attitude, which makes a child ready to listen to his parents, willing to heed their advice, and to follow the guidance of more mature minds. **(Ruth Paxson)**

I am reminded of a sermon by Bob Ferguson on the 23rd Psalm. At the conclusion he tells about a number of people attending a party, one of whom was a renowned actor. After dinner the conversation turned to religion. One of the guests asked the actor to recite the 23rd Psalm. He did. He recited it beautifully and when he finished there were "ohs" and "ahs" and many compliments.

> Also, in attendance there was an elderly or should we say mature minister. After the congratulatory conversation died down the actor very sincerely asked the minister to say the 23rd Psalm and after some encouragement he did so.
>
> When he finished saying *"And I will dwell in the house of the Lord forever"* there was complete silence, there was a hush over the group that lasted a long, long time. Finally, the actor broke the silence saying, "Pastor I know the 23rd Psalm, but you know the Shepherd."
>
> May it be said of us that we know the truth and more importantly that we know the shepherd. **(Robert B. Callahan, Sr.)**

Ruth Paxson tells how on one occasion she was witnessing about God blessing their missionary efforts in China and describing the victories that were realized through the Holy Spirit. She noticed that one person zealously listened to her every word and watched every gesture. Later, the person confessed that they had hoped to catch her in some word or act that would betray her stated commitment to the Lord Jesus Christ. **(Ruth Paxson)**

Mutual subjection is a voluntary meeting on the common ground of mutual desire to do the will of God, in the love of Christ, through the guidance of the Holy Spirit. **(Ruth Paxson)**

What does the Apostle say to the members of Christ's body? Wherever you go, whatever you do, your standard of conduct is to be the Lord Jesus Christ and your relationship to Him. Therefore, if that is the standard, you must learn about Him. You must assimilate His teachings and above all you must come to know Him. **(Robert B. Callahan, Sr.)**

Remember, people are going to judge God, judge the Gospel, and judge Christ by what they see in us. It is an awesome thought! It is an awesome responsibility! Of course, people are wrong to judge in that manner, but they do. While you can not do anything about how they judge you, you can do something about knowing the truth and how you conduct yourself. **(Robert B. Callahan, Sr.)**

It is important to remember when considering the principles described by Paul that our initial reaction may be descent from the lofty, eternal purposes of God to more mundane matters such as personal conduct. The focus of our attention may change from heaven to earth, from the heights of eternity to the realities of every day living, from the sanctity of Christ's life to the darkness of human sin. **(Robert B. Callahan, Sr.)**

There is no room for envy or scorn in it. There is nothing that (fosters) harmony better than this feeling for each other where each one realizes that he is enriched by the benefits of others every bit as much as they, and that when they suffer loss, he is impoverished along with them. **(John Calvin)**

Children may obey their parents in the Lord, before they are able to understand any Christian doctrine; they may discharge every childish duty, under the inspiration of the Spirit of God, before they have so much as heard whether the Spirit of God has been given. **(R.W. Dale)**

Human relationships do not come first; they never come first in the Bible, it is always man's relationship to God first. **(Martyn M. Lloyd-Jones)**

O if ministers only saw the inconceivable glory that is before them, and the preciousness of Christ, they would not be able to refrain from going about leaping and clapping their hands for joy and exclaiming, "I'm a minister of Christ!" When I read Bunyan's description of the land of Beulah where the sun shines and the birds sing day and night I used to doubt whether there were such a place. But now my own experience has convinced me of it, and it infinitely transcends all my previous conceptions. **(Edward Payson)**

The other word is "zoē" which means life, motion, activity. To amplify upon this, it means:

- Life as a principle;
- Life in the absolute sense;
- Life as God has it;
- Life which the Father has in Himself;
- Life which the Father gave to the Son (John 5:26)
- Life, which is not merely a principle of power and mobility but has moral associations which are inseparable from it, as of holiness and righteousness.

  (Robert B. Callahan, Sr.)

The external actions are to exhibit the indwelling Christ and the power of the Holy Spirit. People are changed when they become members of the body of Christ. Probably one of the more famous instances is that of Chuck Colson.

> However, I would like to share another one with you that Martyn Lloyd-Jones told, "An ordinary sort of person lived an evil and dissolute life given to drinking, fighting, foul temper and out of control when drunk. He was known for his flamboyant mustache. He took great pride in it. He did not darken the steps of the church.
>
> Then the unexpected happened –
>
> He went to Church,

> He was converted,
>
> He accepted Jesus as His Lord and Saviour,
>
> He attended church on Sundays and Wednesdays with his very noticeable mustache, which had been the center of his pride and the primary cause of his troubles.
>
> One Sunday he appeared in Church without his mustaches. He had previously referred to them in the plural due to their size.
>
> As he left the sanctuary the minister asked if someone had made a remark about his mustache or had offended him or what had happened.
>
> He responded by saying he had looked in the mirror and saw his two mustaches, recognized what they represented and said, 'them things don't belong to a Christian!' So he cut them and shaved them off."
>
> Oh, that we could cut off the mustaches of our thoughts, our ideas, our attitudes, our acts that don't belong to a real Christian.
>
> Oh, that we would accept Jesus in such a way that we would allow the power to work within and to give us the ability to do as He would have us to do
>
> Oh, that we can put off the old man and all "them things that don't belong to a Christian." **(Martyn Lloyd Jones)**

This is God's battle, we are given the privilege of being in it and of fighting as individual soldiers, but God's honor is involved in it all . . . His glory, and His honor are involved at every point! Be strong in the Lord, remember that He is there and it is His.

Further, the whole movement of salvation is for God's glory; not simply for our deliverance, but for God's glory primarily. **(Martyn Lloyd-Jones)**

He who is to be imitated determines the nature of the imitation. **(Markus Barth)**

If we are children of God, we ought to be imitators of Him. **(John Calvin)**

When a person begins to grow in Christ it does not mean the change will be immediate and complete:
> A violent temper being changed to gentleness, or
>
> Selfishness expanding into generosity, or

A suspicious nature becoming modest, or

The proud person becoming humble, or

The irresponsible becoming responsible.

These changes do not occur without encouragement, support, strength and knowledge which is available only in Christ Jesus. There is always a lag time as evidenced in the parable of the father asking his two sons to work in the field. **(Robert B. Callahan, Sr.)**

Paul shows the origin of the evil life that he describes. The Apostle asserts that you cannot have morality without godliness. There are people who are concerned about morality, but they are not concerned about godliness. **(Robert B. Callahan, Sr.)**

You have inherited the Divine nature, says Peter, now screw your attention down and form habits, give diligence, concentrate. "Add" means all that character means. No man is born either naturally or supernaturally with character, he has to make character. Nor are we born with habits; we have to form habits on the basis of the new life God has put into us . . . Drudgery is the touchstone of character. The great hindrance in spiritual life is that we will look for big things to do. Jesus *"took a towel . . . and began to wash the disciples' feet."* **(Oswald Chambers)**

In Christology the issue is not a change of our consciousness, but the transformation of the realm of lordship and thus of the very structure of life. Jesus Christ is not the object of our knowledge but the giver of new life. Therefore Christology is never just the "knowledge of God the redeemer" but simultaneously the experience of a turning around in our existence. **(Otto Weber)**

While living in the Pittsburgh area we attended the First Presbyterian Church which is located in the heart of the city. It was my privilege to usher in the balcony where an elderly gentleman sat in the same pew every Sunday. He lived at the top of Mt. Washington which is across the Monongahela River from the city. The distance is approximately three to four miles. This gentleman walked that distance twice every Sunday in all types of weather, even in the coldest winter months. One Sunday I said to him "Why don't you take the street car?" He responded, "Bob, I don't have very much money. By walking I can take the street car money and put it in the offering plate." He cast his mite in out of his want, with a joyful heart. (**Robert B. Callahan, Sr.**)

There is to be no root of bitterness, no symptom of wrath, no trace of anger, no echo of clamor, no slime of evil speaking and no dregs of malice remaining in a person, nor seen in one's conduct at any time or place. (**Ruth Paxson**)

Our conversation is to be used for the up-building of the Body of Christ. (**Ruth Paxson**)

The rule governing true stewardship is to carry out the duties faithfully. (**John Calvin**)

He (Paul) tells them (Christ's followers) straightforwardly that they are now part of Christ's body; therefore, they are not to serve men . . . that brings shame or dishonor to God. They are not to perform wicked or shameful acts. Paul wants them to abide with God. Therefore, he wants them to exercise self-control and bring their impulses under rein. (**Robert B. Callahan, Sr.**)

It is the devoutness, charity, uprightness and zeal of the members that contribute to the force and impact of the church, Christ's body, and is exhibited in different ways:

- Integrity and industry;
- Cheerfulness in facing adversity, poverty, and infirmities;
- Faithfulness despite obstacles, temptations, tests and trials;
- Love despite rejection or ill will;
- Obedience, instead of license;
- Growth in knowledge;
- Reverence, not irreverence;
- Caring for others;
- Forgiveness;
- Children in malice, adults in understanding;

- Producing fruit of the Spirit; and
- Refraining from responding to attacks, resentments, injustices, and unkindnesses.

(Robert B. Callahan, Sr.)

We are **self-centered**. We need to become **Christ-centered**! The author of the Epistle to the Hebrews helps us do this saying, that we are to be *looking unto Jesus the author (originator) and finisher (perfector) of our faith*, in order to become Christ-centered. **(Robert B. Callahan, Sr.)**

It is through Christ, having union with Him, and being the beneficiary of His blessings that we become Christ-centered. **(Robert B. Callahan, Sr.)**

If a person does not accept and believe in the grace of God, the person and work of the Lord Jesus Christ, and the power of the Holy Spirit, then that person is not in Christ. **(Robert B. Callahan, Sr.)**

The characteristics of corrupt communications . . . are marked by excesses and lack of self-control. It is when people talk too much and talk without thinking. . . . Their conversations are usually an expression of self. It is self-centered, it focuses on self, it is selfish, and it presents self first and foremost. **(Robert B. Callahan, Sr.)**

The Lord does not discourage us by demanding perfection of character all at once. But our walk should mean a step by step growth in Christlikeness. **(Ruth Paxson)**

We must learn from the whole of life, because the truly wise man is the one who knows how far short he comes of any complete understanding. **(John Calvin)**

The image of God in holiness and righteousness is freeborn in us on the condition of our sharing in eternal life and glory. **(John Calvin)**

Corrupt communications . . . inflame arouse, provoke, corrupt, and produce evil. **(Robert B. Callahan, Sr.)**

If we want to be kept according to the rule which Christ laid down, we must not desire immunity from evils or pray to God to convey us straightway into blessed rest, but must remain content with the certain assurance of victory, and meanwhile resist bravely all the evils from which Christ prayed to His Father that we might have a happy issue. **(John Calvin)**

A Christian (is) to watch . . . that he may keep the Lord's charge and do the duty as imposed upon him as a Christian. This is not a temporary duty, but for his whole lifetime. **(William Gurnall)**

Corrupt communications . . . arouse, provoke corrupt, and produce evil. **(Robert B. Callahan, Sr.)**

We must learn from the whole of life, because the truly wise man is the one who knows how far short he come of any complete understanding. **(John Calvin)**

In Christology the issue is not a change of our consciousness, but the transformation of the realm of Lordship and thus of the very structure of life. Jesus Christ is not the object of our knowledge but the giver of new life. Therefore Christology is never just the "knowledge of God the redeemer" but simultaneously the experience of a turning around in our existence. **(Otto Weber)**

6

CHRIST'S TEACHINGS

Christ particularly has in mind what He did with twelve (12) Apostles, yet He also teaches us, that while we are still novices and weak in faith He will for the time, be gentle, until we grow up into men: so they are wrong who use His times of quiet for self-indulgence which softens the strength of faith. **(John Calvin)**

It is not enough to know all that he has already told us about the Christian life; we must also realize and accept what he is now about to say. It is still part of the whole picture, and his essential teaching. **(Martyn Lloyd-Jones)**

A good and faithful teacher should labor for the upbuilding of the Church. Paul did this. Also, he urged Timothy to reflect on the things that are beneficial to the followers and said, *"If thou put the brethren in remembrance of these things, thou shalt be a good minister of Jesus Christ, nourished up in the words of faith and of good doctrine, whereunto thou hast attained."* [**1 Tim. 4:6**]

Scripture must be the norm for all teaching. It is the only basis for proper teaching and instruction. This means the whole of Scripture, not just selected portions. We need to learn the negatives, as well as the positives, the plusses and the minuses, and what we are to do as well as what we are not to do.

Preachers and teachers are not to continually feed their members and students with milk, liquids and sweets. They are to serve meat, some tough meat, as well as some tart food, and even some vinegar. They are responsible for serving a balanced diet and the hearers are responsible for ingesting it.

Everything cannot be taught at once. However, progress is to be made. Every participant (preacher, teacher, hearer) is to increase in knowledge, understanding, and faith. (**Robert B. Callahan, Sr.**)

Christ preached to them that *"were afar off and to them that were nigh."* This is a very important point. Those who are nigh need the very same message as those who are afar off. Isn't that a blow to some of us? Imagine that we who attend, who worship, who have made a profession of faith need the very same message as those who never darken the doors of a sanctuary. (**Robert B. Callahan, Sr.**)

God's teachings as found in the Scriptures pay us a wonderful compliment. They do not treat us as children or as "nincompoops." They reason with us, they appeal to our understanding, if we will keep an open mind and not let self get in the way. The teaching is reasoned out. This is the process for imparting holiness and sanctification. We should be thankful for it. (**Robert B. Callahan, Sr.**)

Many people believe that once they accept Christ and join the church that their troubles will go away and they will live a life of ease. Further that there will be no fight, there will be no struggle, effort will not be required. So when they find that, on the contrary, they have grave difficulties and in a mighty battle they are utterly discouraged. (**Martyn Lloyd-Jones**)

There is nothing so insidious in the realm of Christendom, nothing so injurious to the body of Christ, nothing further from the teachings of Scripture than that adults do not have to study Christ's teachings and apply themselves to His teachings. No, that is not the teaching of our Master. (**Robert B. Callahan, Sr.**)

They (the New Testament writers) emphasized doctrine, the teachings of Christ, the love of God, the wrath of God, the displeasure of God, the Cross, the shed blood, the sinful nature of man, man's disobedience to God, the need to repent, and the need to practice daily the teachings of the Master. **(Robert B. Callahan, Sr.)**

More than fifty years ago there was an editorial in a publication called the Sunday School Times, which said:

> "Forbidding is as necessary as feeding. There are child psychologists and educators today who would tell us that we must never use "negatives" with a child; tell the children what to do, but never tell them 'don't do this or that;' if we feed the child with positive truth, this is all that is necessary. God does not seem to agree with such worldly wisdom, for His word tells us many things we are not to do, as well as many that we are to do." **(The Sunday School Times)**

I am not as interested in getting through Jude as I am interested in Jude getting through us. **(Chuck Swindoll)**

One human will does not yield to another human will, but both wills are mutually yielded to the will of God in every matter relating to both persons. Mutual subjection is a voluntary meeting on the common ground of mutual desire to do the will of God, in the love of Christ, through the guidance of the Holy Spirit. **(Ruth Paxson)**

Think of it! Men are ignorant of God's, character, His love, and His attributes. . . . They are ignorant of His purposes and His dispensations. They are ignorant of His plan and purpose for the world, the Old and New Testaments, and the will of God. That it is God's world that He controls in His own way; that it is His redemption, restoration and regeneration; that if they die outside Christ they will remain there for eternity; that they are to know the truths of God and the teachings of Christ. I do not intend to be negative, but to state succinctly why a person is being alienated from the life of God. This is an important truth to grasp and understand. **(Robert B. Callahan, Sr.)**

There comes a time when you have to do more than pray. You have to think in Christ. You have to apply the knowledge, understanding, and teachings as they are found in Jesus. (**Robert B. Callahan, Sr.**)

To tell people that what a man believes does not matter as long as he lives a good life and does good is not only a denial of the Gospel, it is bound to discourage people from the only truth which can save them. (**Martyn Lloyd-Jones**)

We are not to be unwilling to hear Him (Christ) speaking by the tongue of men. (**John Calvin**)

7

DISCIPLESHIP

The saints are able bodied men, not by nature, nor by one act of ordination, (e.g. by their baptism), but only in as much as again and again they take up the special armor given to them. Whoever renders service, (shall do it) as one who renders it by the strength which God supplies . . . the armor, or strength, that is "put on" is equated with the "New Man" who is identified with Christ. (**Markus Barth**)

Further, and of great importance, Paul is very concerned that we should have:

- An immediate knowledge of God;
- A real fellowship with Him;
- A personal and intimate relationship;
- A meeting with God;
- That God should be real and personal to us;
- That we should be conscious of His presence; and
- That we should know something of His glory.

   (**Robert B. Callahan, Sr.**)

At times we wonder what has happened when someone makes a profession of faith or becomes very active in the church, then they fade away. They can take the easy step and say they believe, but they have problems with the trials and tribulations of living, with trying to live as Christ would have them to live, with facing the daily challenges, and increasing in knowledge and faith. **(Robert B. Callahan, Sr.)**

By telling them to lay hold upon it, he forbids them to give up or to grow weary in mid-course . . . Nothing has been achieved until we have obtained the future life to which God invites us. **(John Calvin)**

I confess that I do not know, that I cannot understand. I become 'as a little child,' and I look up into the face of Him who is the Way, the Truth, and the Life! But from the moment you enter it in that way you begin to use your understanding, and it grows and develops, and there is literally no end to it. **(Martyn Lloyd-Jones)**

The disciples were to grow in strength, faith, and obedience. So are we! The Lord Jesus will be gentle and loving with us and even protective, so that we will not be exposed to certain hardships, conflicts, and strife before our condition has received ample strength and enlightenment. "Christ particularly has in mind what He did with the twelve apostles, yet He also teaches us, that while we are still novices and weak in faith He will for the time, be gentle, until we grow up into men: so they are wrong who use His times of quiet for self-indulgence which softens the strength of faith. **(John Calvin)**

What happens when we "walk as children of light?" There is fruit and it is evident in goodness, righteousness, and truth. There are certain characteristics about fruit. It does not appear overnight and it is not stamped out, or fabricated, or ready made. **(Robert B. Callahan, Sr.)**

There is nothing in scripture which may not contribute to your instruction and the training of your life. **(John Calvin)**

The greatest saints have always testified to the fierceness of the battle, to their own weakness, to their own inability. **(Martyn Lloyd-Jones)**

We need to be careful and accurate about every step we take as members of Christ's body. A vivid description of how we are to walk is contained in Bishop Moule's words, "The appeal is again for a grave remembrance that a walk in the light is no mere promenade, smooth and easy, but a march, resolved and full of purpose, cautious against the enemy, watchful for opportunity for the King, and self controlled in every habit, and possible only in the power of the eternal Spirit." **(Bishop Moule)**

God has told us we would have temptations, trials, testings, so we must be prepared to stand the strain of the slippery paths of temptation and the stony hills of adversity and affliction . . . as we walk through this disordered world there are a thousand things to bruise and wound us. **(Ruth Paxson)**

Paul was subject to many indignities. Many of us have experienced embarrassments or been ashamed of some word or deed. Undoubtedly, Paul was concerned about this and had sought an answer from God. Augustine helps illuminate this matter saying, "For this should be borne in mind . . . , for if they have defects mixed with their virtues, if they are persecuted out of hatred, if they are attacked with curses, these are not merely the rods of their heavenly instructor, but the buffetings which are designed to restrain all haughtiness and fill them with modesty. Therefore let all godly men take note. What a dreadful poison pride is, so that the only antidote to it is another poison." **(St. Augustine)**

What then is it? It is our relationship to God and His Son, Christ Jesus.

> The gospel says, *made nigh*. It does not say have improved, or the conduct is proper, or the morality is impeccable, or the attendance is 100%, or the giving has increased, or the behavior is better. No, it says, *made nigh by the blood of Christ*. **(Robert B. Callahan, Sr.)**

Zeal needs to be governed and controlled by reasoning, understanding, and wisdom. **(Ruth Paxson)**

It is unthinkable for the followers of Christ to live as the non-believers do. Your whole life and behavior, your demeanor and deportment should bear witness to being a member of the body of Christ. People should know that we are different and that we have so learned Christ. **(Robert B. Callahan, Sr.)**

Over and above everything else, our ultimate, our final consideration is our desire to seek, to know, and to discover the will of the Lord in order that we may please Him. It is this personal relationship to this blessed person. (**Martyn Lloyd-Jones**)

The New Testament emphasizes one main point that is dramatically opposed to the way most church members think, and that is the New Testament does not emphasize what we do, but what we are and what we are to become. (**Robert B. Callahan, Sr.**)

What our duty is when confronted by enemies or undesirable circumstances. We should continually pursue our duty, our responsibility as Christ's disciples. We are "To seek help at the hands of God" and be "not dismayed" nor diverted . . . from . . . our duty." (**John Calvin**)

Disciples hesitated at first until Christ approached them nearer and more intimately. When they knew him in truth and certainty, then they worshipped Him. There is no doubt that his approach to them took away all doubts. Before relating that the office of teaching was laid upon them, Matthew says that Christ spoke first of His power, and rightly so . . . The Apostles would never be persuaded to undertake such a task of difficulty unless they knew that their Champion sat in heaven, and that supreme power was given to him. (**John Calvin**)

However, Paul, Peter, John and the other New Testament authors wrote about doctrine and deep spiritual truths. They wanted the people to know and to understand the truth of Christ. If it was urgent to those who had seen and heard the Lord Jesus during his ministry then it should also be with us. It seems that one thing we should be able to learn is the urgency of the truths presented in Scripture. (**Robert B. Callahan, Sr.**)

That there is much less ground for tolerating the ignorance of people who think the Gospel is offered universally to all men in such a way that it is free to everyone without distinction to lay hold of salvation by faith. (**John Calvin**)

A mission station and hospital in China had problems, unrest, and disobedience.

Then there was a revival as a result of preaching and teaching the word and the Holy Spirit working among the people.

The missionary wrote our hospital is no more like it used to be. There is perfect harmony among all the hospital workers from servants up. All do faithful work. I never have to reprove any of them. I even never have to tell servants what to do. All know their work and do it faithfully. **(Ruth Paxson)**

"Am I a Solider of the Cross"

Am I a soldier of the cross,
A follower of the Lamb,
And shall I fear to own His cause,
Or blush to speak His name?

Must I be carried to the skies,
On flowery beds of ease,
While others fought to win the prize,
And sailed through bloody seas?

Are there no foes for me to face?
Must I not stem the flood?
Is this vile world a friend to grace,
To help me on to God?

Sure I must fight, if I would reign;
Increase my courage Lord;
I'll bear the toil, endure the pain,
Supported by thy Word.
(Isaac Watts)

The image of God in holiness and righteousness is reborn in us on the condition of our sharing in eternal life and glory. **(John Calvin)**

We should appreciate the fact that a pure, candid, and straightforward presentation of sound doctrine is required from Christ's servants. As Paul said, *If thou put the brethren in remembrance of these things, thou shalt be a good minister of Jesus Christ.* [**1 Tim 4:6**] **(Robert B. Callahan, Sr.)**

On no one has God bestowed all things, but each has received a certain measure, so that we need one another; and by bringing together what is given to them individually, they help one another. **(John Calvin)**

Ernest Logan, an Irishman, . . . an associate minister at the First Presbyterian Church in Pittsburgh would ask individuals joining the Church about their Christian experiences He would listen patiently as they talked about their lives as children and growing up in a fine home, about the various jobs or functions they had performed in the churches to which they had belonged, or about the boards on which they had served.

Then Ernest would say, "Aye that is all very well and good, but would ye mind telling me about your relationship with the Lord Jesus Christ? Usually this question caused consternation and long pauses before responding. Ernest had a way of cutting to the heart of the matter. It is our relationship with Christ that is important, nothing more, nothing less, nothing else. **(Robert B. Callahan, Sr.)**

There are three major impediments hindering growth in the faith and serving Christ as his disciples. They are the secular world, false preaching and teaching, and the unrelenting attacks of Satan. **(Robert B. Callahan, Sr.)**

To put on Christ means . . . to be defended on every side by the power of His Spirit, and thus rendered fit to discharge all the duties of holiness. **(John Calvin)**

True love of Christ is really determined by keeping His teachings and being obedient unto Him. **(Robert B. Callahan, Sr.)**

"Soldiers of Christ, Arise"

Soldiers of Christ arise,
And put your armor on.
Strong in the strength which God supplies
through His eternal Son'
Strong in the Lord of hosts,
and in his mighty power;
Who in the strength of Jesus trusts

Is more than conqueror.

Stand then in His great might
With all His strength endued,
And take to arm you for the fight,
The panoply of God;
That having all things done,
And all your conflicts past,
Ye o'ercome through Christ alone,
And stand entire at last.

Leave no unguarded place,
No weakness of the soul;
Take every virtue, every grace,
And fortify the whole.
From strength to strength go on,

Wrestle and fight and pray,
Tread all the powers of darkness down,
And win the well fought day.
(Charles Wesley)

But on the other side of the coin our faith is to correspond to our love and works. Yes you may have or you should fulfill your obligations to men, but, and this important, you are to apply yourself, "with no less zeal to progress in your faith, so as to show God its full and firm certainty. **(John Calvin)**

There was a gentleman who had lived in New York City for many years and had applied for membership in the prestigious New York Yacht Club. Every morning he would walk by the Yacht Club and say good morning cheerfully to the doorman, but he never ever received a response to his greeting during the time his application was being considered. Late one evening the membership committee looked favorably upon his application, since there was an opening and they accepted him as a member. The next morning he followed his customary route to his office and as he approached the New York Yacht Club the doorman beamed, smiled and heartily said, "Good morning Mr. Jones." Why? Because now he was a member of the Yacht Club, he was acceptable, he was looked upon with favor and he had all the rights and privileges of membership. **(Robert B. Callahan, Sr.)**

We walk as pilgrims in an unregenerate world. All around us is gross spiritual and moral darkness, the dazzling light of the ... wisdom of man. We walk as Christians in the midst of an apostate church, wherein the world, the flesh and the devil have been allowed great liberty in dictating its plans and in the control of its programs. In no period of church history was God's exhortation, *See then that ye walk circumspectly*{carefully} {Eph. 5:15}, *not as fools, but as wise,* more needed than today.

Character determines conduct; therefore live, speak, act as sons of light .... It is inconceivable that the walk of children of darkness and children of light should be the same in any particular. Everything in the walk of the Christian should be differentiated from that of the sinner. There is a walk that becometh sinners, but such a walk is unbefitting saints, even to its minutest details. Our conduct and our conversation betray us, for they reveal the kingdom in which we are citizens. **(Ruth Paxson)**

Man is not to be controlled by his instincts; he is to be controlled by God and to be obedient to His commands and teachings. **(Robert B. Callahan, Sr.)**

8

FAITH

Faith seeks understanding. **(Anselm)**

Paul never speaks of a faith that is quietistic in regard to ethics, and passive in situations that demand decisions and action. **(Karl Barth)**

We cannot completely and fully understand all the truths of God as we begin and proceed on our journey of faith. God's truths are revealed to us along the way, as we are able to grasp and understand them. We are not fully capable of understanding all that God knows, but we are capable of increasing in faith and wisdom. **(Robert B. Callahan, Sr.)**

Paul's faith was expressed in revealing the great truths of God, in presenting the Lord Jesus Christ and making Him known to the followers. It was expressed in assuring them of the real tenderness yet at the same time the unsurpassable strength of the love of God and His manifold wisdom in providing for our salvation. This was Paul's faith. It was part and parcel of his invincible energy and contagious enthusiasm. **(Robert B. Callahan, Sr.)**

This faith brings me to the person of Jesus Christ just as I am, as myself, without my defenses, or my ego. It reveals me unprotected and insecure. I cannot surround myself with my past, my desires, my profession, my intentions, my relationships, my comparisons, or anything else. My believing is not based upon this world, but my faith redirects every part of me toward this world, the people and things that surround me. (**Robert B. Callahan, Sr.**)

There is an interesting fact here. We have faith only as we receive it. And we have baptism only as we receive it. Faith and baptism belong together. However, baptism does not result from faith and faith does not result from baptism. (**Robert B. Callahan, Sr.**)

Anyone who has the firm conviction that he will never be forsaken by the Lord will not be unduly anxious because he will depend on His providence. (**John Calvin**)

The Apostle John, by many arguments proves that faith is joined to a holy and pure life. First that we are spiritually begotten in the likeness of Christ. From this it follows that no one is born of Christ save He who lives righteously. (**John Calvin**)

What does God's faithfulness do? It calls forth our faith, it strengthens our faith, and it allows us to grasp our faith. (**Robert B. Callahan, Sr.**)

A trembling, hesitating, doubting conscience will always be sure proof of unbelief, but a firm, steady conscience, victorious against the gates of hell, will be sure proof of faith. To trust in Christ as Mediator, and to rest with assurance in God's fatherly love, to dare boldly to promise our selves eternal life, and not to tremble at death or hell, this is, as they say, a holy presumption. (**John Calvin**)

When contemplating this teaching we must recognize what Christ is stressing in this passage. Not that faith is the gift of God and that we may use it or not, but that faith is what God requires of us, and He wants us to exhibit it daily. (**Robert B. Callahan, Sr.**)

Paul declares that faith which rests upon the Word of God stands unshaken against all the attacks of Satan. (**John Calvin**)

For it is certain that faith cannot stand, unless it is founded on the promises of God. *God promises, blesses and fulfills.* (**John Calvin**)

Calvin says that the Apostle John, "By many arguments proves that faith is joined to a holy and pure life. First that we are spiritually begotten in the likeness of Christ. From this it follows that no one is born of Christ save He who lives righteously." **(John Calvin)**

There are two kinds of assurance: The first rests on the promises of God, so that the believer is convinced in his heart that God will never leave him, and relying on this unconquerable conviction he stands up to Satan and sin, cheerful and undaunted. At the same time, however, remembering his own weakness, he falls back on God in fear and humility, and in his anxiety willingly commits himself to Him. This kind of assurance is a holy thing, and cannot be separated from faith. **(John Calvin)**

God makes trial of our faith in this way, . . . that we become partakers with Christ. **(John Calvin)**

It was given to strengthen us, to build us up in our most holy faith. However, our faith cannot be strengthened, we cannot be built up if we do not partake of the food, if we don't go to where the food is being served, if we don't take time to eat, remember who we are and our relationship to God and to Christ. **(Martyn Lloyd-Jones)**

Faith begins with a ready and willing desire to obey God's commands. However, . . . some people exhibit a willingness at the beginning, but they do not persevere. **(Robert B. Callahan, Sr.)**

Faith makes us friendly to God. **(Robert B. Callahan, Sr.)**

Faith enables us to read Scripture, to hear it, and to know that it is God who is speaking. Faith enables a person to believe God's Word, to fully accept it, and to depend upon it. When a person comes to believe it, then he begins to pray for it. **(Robert B. Callahan, Sr.)**

Those who live after the flesh may boast of justification by faith, but they are doing so without the Spirit of Christ. Further, where there is no confidence in God, then there is no love of righteousness. **(Robert B. Callahan, Sr.)**

For it is certain that faith can not stand, unless it is founded on the promises of God. **(John Calvin)**

The problem is that these people do not have a clear understanding of the Christian faith. They have an utterly inadequate notion of what Christianity means. Their idea of Christianity was or is: Believe in Christ and you will never have another trouble or problem; God will bless you; [and] nothing will ever go wrong with you. **(Martyn Lloyd-Jones)**

Hope is a supernatural gift of God, whereby the believer, through Christ, expects and waits for all those good things of the promise, which at present he hath not received, or not fully. **(William Gurnall)**

Again and again we are reminded it is relatively easy to accept Christ by faith. But, it is very difficult to *walk in love, as Christ also hath loved us.* **(Robert B. Callahan, Sr.)**

The godly calmly wait for Christ and do not dread His presence. **(John Calvin)**

God requires of us only that we believe. There is an implied contrast between faith and men's cares and efforts here, as if He were saying men are busied to no purpose when they try to please God without faith. **(John Calvin)**

The New Testament epistles were written not to tell us how to live a life of ease, but how to withstand the pressures, subtleties, disappointments, defeats, and failures of life and to be *more than conquerors* in Christ. **(Robert B. Callahan, Sr.)**

Assurance from God produces humility, whereas man's assurance in himself produces pride. **(Robert B. Callahan, Sr.)**

Unbelief is always proud and a despiser of God. **(John Calvin)**

Justification is by faith, but assurance, confidence, and trust come from worshipping, acquiring knowledge, and practicing the commandments. **(Robert B. Callahan, Sr.)**

God's assurance produces a hunger and thirst for righteousness and for knowledge of the Master. Certainly, it does not produce self-satisfaction, complacency, indifference, or apostasy. (**Robert B. Callahan, Sr.**)

Luther's heart and mind were opened, and "He saw that the righteousness of God is given through faith and that it is something which can be received immediately." (**Martyn Lloyd-Jones**)

From avarice can come the greatest evil of all—-apostasy from the faith. (**Robert B. Callahan, Sr.**)

This is a very fine passage, and from it we can plainly see how great is the blindness of the human mind, which surrounded by light, perceives nothing. For it is true that the world is like a theatre in which the Lord shows to us a striking spectacle of His glory. However, when such a sight lies open before our eyes, we are quite blind, not because the revelation is obscure, but because we are alienated in mind, meaning that not only the will but also the power for this activity fails us. For notwithstanding that God shows Himself openly, yet it is only by the eye of faith that we can look at Him, bearing in mind that we receive only a slight inkling as to His divine nature, but enough to put us in the position of being without excuse. (**John Calvin**)

You must now apply yourself with not less zeal to progress in your faith, so as to show God its firm and full certainty. (**John Calvin**)

Godliness and the sincere worship of God cannot be separated from faith. (**John Calvin**)

Should any man imitate his patience, no doubt he will likewise feel the hand of God come at last to his relief . . . God did not allow his servant Job to be vanquished for he endured his pains with patience: So the patience of no man will be wasted . . . Why does the Apostle so greatly commend the patience of Job, who . . . showed considerable signs of impatience. The answer is, that even though on occasion he lapses through weakness of the flesh, . . . yet he always comes back to entrusting himself wholly to God, and offering himself to his restraining and controlling arm. (**John Calvin**)

There can be no genuine assurance before God unless His spirit produces in us the fruit of love. **(John Calvin)**

Faith comes when it has deep roots in the heart and builds on a base of serious and enduring commitments, which yield less and less to temptations. **(Robert B. Callahan, Sr.)**

Faith is not merely an in intellectual assent; it involves the whole personality. It not only involves the mind, but the heart and the will and therefore every aspect of practice and behavior. **(Martyn Lloyd-Jones)**

What comes first is our faith in the Lord Jesus:
> Not our conduct;
> Not our moral behavior;
> Not being good;
> Not being benevolent;
> Not anything we do;
> Not what we think;
> Not what other people think about us;
> Not our ability;
> Not our accomplishments;
> Not working on committees; and
> Not a person's character.
> **(Robert B. Callahan, Sr.)**

Assurance is rather the fruit of faith, than faith itself. It is in faith as the flower is in the root. Faith, in time, after much communion with God, acquaintance with the word, and experience of his dealings with the soul, may flourish into assurance. But, as the root truly lives before the flower appears, and continues when that hath shed its beautiful leaves, and is gone again; so doth true justifying faith live before assurance comes, and after it disappears. **(William Gurnall)**

The essential thing is my personal relationship to Jesus Christ–that I may know him. To fulfill God's design means, complete abandonment to Him. Whenever I want things for myself, the relationship is distorted. It will be a big humiliation to realize that I have not been concerned about realizing Jesus Christ, but only about realizing what He has done for me. **(Oswald Chambers)**

Contrary to popular opinion, the life in Christ is one of demands, requirements, obedience, and fighting the good fight of faith. It is not a life of ease and rest, where you go merrily on your way. **(Robert B. Callahan, Sr.)**

Christ's words show that nothing relating to the Holy Spirit can be learned from human reason, but that He is known only by the experience in faith. **(John Calvin)**

A sense of wonder, amazement, and surprise. In other words, the true Christian does not say, 'Of course I am saved.' He says, it is an amazing thing that I should be saved at all. How did the almighty God ever bring Himself to look upon me? **(Martyn Lloyd-Jones)**

The secret of Abraham was that his faith led him to God, and God's character and promises; and when he relied upon them, all was well.

We are told about the great heroes of the faith in Hebrews 11, that out of weakness they were made strong; always by faith! Not faith in faith, but faith in God! They were men who believed God, they accounted him able to do that which he had promised. That was their secret. **(Martyn Lloyd-Jones)**

Christians might avoid much trouble and inconvenience if they would only believe what they profess, that God is able to make them happy without anything else. They imagine that if such a dear friend were to die, or if such blessings were to be removed, they would be miserable, whereas God can make them a thousand times happier without them. To mention my own case, God has been depriving me of one blessing after another (he was on his death bed when he wrote this), but as each one was removed He has come in and filled its place. And now, when I am a cripple and not able to move, I am happier than ever I was in my life before or ever expected to be; and if I had believed this twenty years ago I might have been spared much anxiety. **(Edward Payson)**

Faith is the way of access unto God through an act of believing in the Lord Jesus Christ, who is the heart of the faith. **(Ruth Paxson)**

The faithfulness of God himself and the faithful service of the one who is anointed by God. The good fight of faith could not be fought by any man if man had to rely upon his own faith: *I believe: help thou my unbelief* [Mark 9:24]. *The "faith" to which "victory over the world* is given is as much "born from God" [1 John 5:4] as the brotherly love among men is founded upon and preceded by the love of God for men. [1 John 4:10, 19]. **(Markus Barth)**

Though undaunted, he was not self-confident. He needed strength and courage . . . to faithfully fulfill his duties. **(Ruth Paxson)**

And can it be, that I should gain an interest in the Saviour's blood? Died He for me, who caused His Pain? For me, who Him to death pursued? Amazing love! How can it be, that thou, my God, should die for me? **(Charles Wesley)**

It is the I-Thou relation, which is what faith in fact is, [it] is by analogy a response to and a taking of responsibility for God's personal relation to man. However, God is the Creator. **(Otto Weber)**

Faith prompts the believer to discover the lives of the saints who have gone before, who have had to overcome difficulties, obstacles and temptations. **(Robert B. Callahan, Sr.)**

It is only when we embrace what we are taught calmly, gladly and with one mind, that we are really prepared for faith. **(John Calvin)**

The Apostle John presents a great truth. Christ's followers are enlightened by the Spirit for one simple and great reason: So they may know Christ. He promised that the fruit of their perseverance would be boldness, and they would not be ashamed of His presence. Faith is not apprehensive about Christ, but has a living and vital sense of His presence and His power which begets confidence. How true this is! Faith must be fixed upon Christ and in turn is supported by His power which produces confidence. This confidence boldly bears the presence of Christ. Those who have faith and in whom faith increases calmly wait for Christ and rejoice in His presence. **(Robert B. Callahan, Sr.)**

These verses (Eph. 4:22–24) are "the crossroads between God's sovereign work through grace and man's cooperative action through faith." **(Ruth Paxson)**

Hope is a supernatural grace of God, whereby the believer, through Christ expects and waits for all those good things of the promise, which at present he hath not received, or not fully. **(William Gurnall)**

"Will this faith ever carry thee to heaven that is not able to bring thee out of hell?" **(William Gurnall)**

A religion may not be needed, but a living faith is a necessity. **(Robert B. Callahan, Sr.)**

Faith takes away the fuel that feeds . . . temptation. **(William Gurnall)**

It is the supreme achievement of reason to show that there is a limit to reason. **(Blaise Pascal)**

Faith is human behavior. God does not "believe" nor does the Holy Spirit "believe." We believe. The New Testament speaks primarily of the faith which man has, not what God has. **(Otto Weber)**

Faith has two basic truths. First, it has a 'confident reliance on God. It is the act by which he lays hold on God's proffered resources and becomes obedient to what God prescribes. Further, it abandons all self-interest and self-reliance, and trusts God completely. Second, it is the Old Testament truth whereby "a person who has faith is himself made firm and reliable. However, it is God's act that brings about 'loyalty to God which is found in a man of faith.' Further, God brings about within a person a belief that is firm and trustworthy, even though the individual previously had been helpless and unstable. **(W.A. Whitehouse)**

Faith provides the believer with the ability to apply quickly what we believe so as to repel everything the devil does or attempts to do to us.

Faith is not merely an intellectual belief or theory. . . . Faith is always practical. **(Martyn Lloyd-Jones)**

Paul believing in the *"unsearchable riches of Christ,"* knew that:
- For human sin there is divine forgiveness;
- For human weakness there is divine redemption;
- For human uncertainty and doubt there is divine illumination;
- For human fears and needs there is free access to God; and
- For human limitations and restless discontent there is ineffable strength, righteousness and mercy in our union with the Lord Jesus Christ.

(Robert B. Callahan, Sr.)

In understanding faith it is not merely a question of knowing that God exists, but . . . of knowing his will toward us. **(John Calvin)**

The people identified in this magnificent chapter (Hebrews 11:13) embraced the promises of faith. It does not say that they embraced them easily, readily, quickly or glibly. Notice this verse says, having seen them afar off, and were persuaded of them. They were persuaded. But, these people had their questions, their trials, and their tests. However, they had faith and they embraced the promises. **(Robert B. Callahan, Sr.)**

Calvin expresses it very well saying that as we consider the meaning of faith we "ought to contemplate what is exhibited to us in Christ." A bare and confused knowledge about God must not be taken for faith. But, true faith can be realized only when the power and office of Christ are understood. Possibly, this can be better illustrated by stating that first there is an initial confidence, then progress, and finally boldness. This occurs in the following manner:

> Believing in God's promises, developing confidence in them, acquiring by the grace of God the proper mind-set, generating boldness, and entrusting ourselves courageously and steadfastly to God.

This does not happen in the twinkling of an eye or overnight. It requires a life time of allowing God to work in us through the Holy Spirit. (**Robert B. Callahan, Sr.**)

Faith does not rest on ignorance, but on knowledge. It is not the authority of the church, nor the power of emotional involvement that establishes and preserves faith. The knowledge to be obtained is the self-disclosure of God through the Lord Jesus Christ. (**Robert B. Callahan, Sr.**)

Why does Paul tie faith and love together? Because faith works by love, faith is energized by love, a life of faith is active because of love. (**Robert B. Callahan, Sr.**)

Faith is joined to a holy and pure life. Further, the Apostle teaches that no one is born of Christ except those who live or strive to live righteously. We who are born of Christ are renewed by His Spirit. (**John Calvin**)

The good works are the fruit, but not the automatic product of faith. The good works being discussed result from the act of justification. They are not equal to it. (**Otto Weber**)

Because some professing faith in Christ were being distracted by opinions, superstitions, doubts, and false teachings. The author of Hebrews points out that the truth of God is unwavering. Since it is the faith of those who rely upon Him and they are members of the community of believers, they should be true, sure, firm, and above all have no doubts. (**Robert B. Callahan, Sr.**)

When men abandon themselves to unrestrained license they remove all barriers between good and evil, pleasing and displeasing God, and righteousness and unrighteousness. (**John Calvin**)

The great enemy of the life of faith in God is not sin, but the good which is not good enough. The good is always the enemy of the best. (**Oswald Chambers**)

Our souls are fed by the teaching of the Gospel, when it is efficacious by the power of the Spirit. Therefore, as faith is the life of the soul, all that nourishes and advances faith is compared to food. **(John Calvin)**

It is not only that faith is the gift of God and that we may use it or not, but that faith is what God requires of us. He wants us to exhibit it daily, in all the phases of our lives. **(Robert B. Callahan, Sr.)**

The Lord in no way measures his precepts according to our strength, or the power of free will, nor does he instruct us in our duty, so that we may place reliance on our own powers and prepare ourselves to render obedience. Rather, the precepts which he gives us require the assistance of His grace to stimulate us to an assiduous desire for prayer . . . It is only when we embrace what we are taught calmly, gladly and with one mind, that we are really prepared for faith. **(John Calvin)**

Faith is holding on to what you believe to be true, despite your emotions. **(C. S. Lewis)**

Those who are righteousness by faith are righteous outside themselves, that is in Christ. **(John Calvin)**

When Christ tells Nicodemus not to marvel, He means that we should not shake our heads in disbelief and as a result impede our faith, but we should admire the work of God. Further, we should never doubt for a moment that by the power of God and the workings of the Holy Spirit that we are re-fashioned and made new. However, the way God does this is not revealed to us. **(Robert B. Callahan, Sr.)**

But, on the other side of the coin our faith is to correspond to our love and works. Yes, you may have or you should fulfill your obligations to men, but, and this is important, you are to apply yourself, "with no less zeal to progress in your faith, so as to show God its full and firm certainty." **(John Calvin)**

Faith is not apprehensive about Christ, but has a living and vital sense of His presence and power, which begets confidence. How true this is! Faith must be fixed upon Christ and in turn is supported by His power, which produces confidence. This confidence boldly bears the presence of Christ. Those who have faith and in whom faith increases calmly wait for Christ and rejoice in His presence. **(Robert B. Callahan, Sr.)**

Faith does not depend on our own decision, it is given by God. **(Robert B. Callahan, Sr.)**

Those who *live after the flesh* may boast of justification by faith, but they are doing so without the Spirit of Christ. **(Robert B. Callahan, Sr.)**

This reminds me of an experience at the First Presbyterian Church in Pittsburgh; while participating in a Bible study class. It was an in-depth study that progressed during twelve weeks from milk and soft foods to tough meat. The course focused on the Lord Jesus Christ and His teachings. There was a lady in the group who was obviously struggling and having difficulty learning Christ and the truth as it is in Him. This went on for a number of weeks. She was what you may describe as a nominal Christian. One night near the end of the class after a certain amount of discussion the Holy Spirit enlightened her and she exclaimed, "Now I know and understand that Jesus is My Lord, My God!" **(Robert B. Callahan, Sr.)**

Such is Satan's enmity and envy against a Christian's joy and comfort, that he cannot but act to the utmost of his life to keep poor souls in doubt and darkness. Satan knows that assurance is a pearl of that price that will make the soul happy forever; he knows that assurance makes a Christian's wilderness to be a paradise; he knows that assurance begets in Christians that most noble and generous spirits; he knows that assurance is that which will make men strong to do exploits, to shake his tottering kingdom about his ears; and therefore he is very studious and industrious to keep souls from assurance, as he was to cast Adam out of Paradise. **(Thomas Brooks)**

Faith makes us friendly to God. By faith God washes away our sins and restores us to His image. **(Robert B. Callahan, Sr.)**

Faith is human behavior. God does not "believe" nor does the Holy Spirit "believe." We believe the New Testament speaks primarily of the faith which man has, not what God has. (**Otto Weber**)

By telling them to lay hold upon it (eternal life), he forbids them to give up or grow weary in mid-course . . . . Nothing has been achieved until we have obtained the future life to which God invites us. (**John Calvin**)

Godliness and the sincere worship of God cannot be separated from faith. (**John Calvin**)

Where is that simple, easy faith that does not require much of me? It is not in the New Testament. The New Testament is filled with conflict, rejection and opposition in addition to love, mercy, and righteousness. (**Robert B. Callahan, Sr.**)

9

FORGIVENESS

If we do not forgive, then Satan will take advantage of us. People are willing to forgive the preacher, at times, or certain people. However, our Lord never put any limits on forgiveness. We are to forgive and to accept the repentant sinner. People can talk about love, about God, about Christ, but if they do not truly and sincerely extend and bestow forgiveness upon others, all others, without limitation, then they are not doing the will of the Father, nor are they obeying the commands of the Lord Jesus Christ. **(Robert B. Callahan, Sr.)**

Redemption is ultimately going to end in the glorification of my body; but it begins with forgiveness and continues to emphasize it. **(Martyn Lloyd-Jones)**

For if ye forgive men their trespasses, your heavenly Father will also forgive you: For if ye forgive not men their trespasses, neither will your Father forgive your trespasses. [**Matthew 6:14-15**]

You will note in John's statement that the Apostle says *"from all sin."* Though we are guilty on many counts and have many faults, God forgives us and through His forgiveness finds us pleasing. Consequently, our sins do not prevent us from pleasing Him since we have been cleansed by the blood of Christ. It is the cleansing power of Christ's blood that makes us acceptable to God. **(Robert B. Callahan, Sr.)**

The reason He did not spare His own Son was that you and I might not be forgiven. **(Martyn Lloyd-Jones)**

It is Christ crucified, and the fact He was crucified for me that results in my debt being paid, my being pardoned, and my receiving eternal life. **(Robert B Callahan, Sr.)**

Though we are guilty on many counts and have many faults God forgives us and through His forgiveness we become pleasing to Him. Consequently, our sins do not prevent us from pleasing Him since we have been cleansed by the blood of Christ. It is the cleansing power of Christ's blood that makes us acceptable to God. **(Robert B. Callahan, Sr.)**

10

GOD, THE FATHER

Even though God confronts us on one side, He does even more. He supports the other side through the Lord Jesus Christ. As we consider analogies let us remember one thing, there is no way there can be an analogy from the creature back to the Creator. It is only from the Creator to the creature. Further, it is in the Lord Jesus Christ that God, the Creator, comes to us and dwells among us. Even though He dwells among us He still remains the Creator. (**Robert B. Callahan, Sr.**)

For it is not so much our concern to know who he is in himself, as what he wills to be toward us. (**John Calvin**)

The Father, himself infinite, becomes finite in the Son, for he has accommodated himself to our little measure lest our minds be overwhelmed by the immensity of his glory. (**John Calvin**)

In the Bible clouds are always connected with God [or Christ]. If there were no clouds, we should have no faith or no hope. The clouds are a sign that He is there . . . God cannot come near without clouds, He does not come in clear sunshine. (**Oswald Chambers**)

Make no mistake about this, the truth of God is something that is to be experienced. It is not a philosophical system, it is not a mere ethical teaching. The whole object and end of the Christian (faith) is to bring us to a knowledge of God; and God is not some kind of philosophic 'X.'

He is not an abstraction, a mere postulate in philosophy. God is! He is a personal deity. And He is to be known. **(Martyn Lloyd-Jones)**

I confess that I do not know, that I cannot understand. I become 'as a little child,' and I look up into the face of Him who is the Way, the Truth, and the Life! But from the moment you enter it in that way you begin to use your understanding, and it grows and develops, and there is literally no end to it. **(Martyn Lloyd-Jones)**

With God there (are) no surprises and no emergencies. The Word made flesh was not an afterthought of God. (His) eternal purpose encompasses God's relationship to the saints and faithful, and how they (you and me) are to become like him and be with him now and forever. **(Ruth Paxson)**

God is the fountain of love. That this affection flows from God and is poured out where there is knowledge of Him. **(John Calvin)**

He (God) confronts us as one who can be confused or exchanged with no other. **(Otto Weber)**

We fail to recognize God in that we are not willing to accept that he is good to us. We fail to recognize in ourselves that we are not willing to accept [the truth] that we should submit ourselves to him. **(Otto Weber)**

Think of it this way:
> The presence of God–abides
> The plenitude of God–abounds
> The power of God–achieves. **(John Calvin)**

We are only able to understand the knowledge of God as we (do), did (or will) because God himself discloses and has disclosed Himself as a person: In Jesus Christ through the Holy Spirit. **(Otto Weber)**

Patiently God, through our history, accommodates his ways of revelation to our condition. Thus, par excellence, the Word made flesh and the written Word from which he speaks is God accommodating himself to us. **(Ford Lewis Battles)**

What we most need to know about God can come only from God, and it does come through God's self-disclosure in the incarnate Word and the written Word; . . . furthermore, that self-disclosure is typically couched in terms accommodated to the limits of human capacity. **(Roland Frye)**

Remember, it was God who called Abraham and formed the nation of Israel. It was God who took the action. Man, all men need to be reconciled to God. Therefore, God singled out Abraham and established a nation to be witnesses. But the question is why did He do it? So that He might have fellowship with Abraham, Israel and their descendants, and that they might have fellowship with Him. The Gentiles and others were not in fellowship with Him at that time. This is an important truth to grasp in order to understand the Old Testament. God formed a peculiar people for Himself and for the relationship between them. **(Robert B. Callahan, Sr.)**

On no one has God bestowed all things, but each has received a certain measure, so that we need one another; and by bringing together what is given to them individually, they help one another. **(John Calvin)**

The greatest triumph, which God ever won was when Christ, after subduing sin, conquering death, and putting Satan to flight rose majestically to heaven, that He might exercise His glorious reign over the church. **(John Calvin)**

We do not know the full and complete answer. However, if God had not allowed the possibility of man's fall then there would have been limitations on man's freedom. If there had been limitations, man would not have been created perfectly by God. Man as created by God had free will but he lost it by falling into sin. However, no matter what the explanation, it is perfectly clear that God has overruled it through His redemption and in so doing, has displayed certain attributes of His Holy being, nature, and character. Otherwise these things would never have been known. **(Robert B. Callahan, Sr.)**

From God's promise to dwell among us we may infer that He also remains in us. **(John Calvin)**

However severe and wrathful a judge God shows Himself to be towards unbelievers (and believers) whenever He punishes them, His primary purpose is to provide counsel for their salvation and to have them come into a right relationship with Himself. This is one way by which He demonstrates His fatherly love. **(John Calvin)**

Isn't it a thrilling thought that we are being fashioned and made by God in Christ? This catches us by surprise. Our whole background and mindset is that we have joined the church, we have made a profession of faith, we attend church, we pray, we read Scripture. We think of ourselves as being active and of God as being passive. We think God waits until we do something. However, it is God who pricks us and causes us to act. He is the active one and we are passive until He acts in us. **(Robert B. Callahan, Sr.)**

God does not communicate to us empty fiction. **(John Calvin)**

God glorified His Son while He was on earth.
> He gave Him power to perform miracles,
> He gave Him words to speak,
> He glorified His death,
> He glorified His resurrection,
> He gives His glory to His Son,
> He gives His glory to others, and
> He gives His glory to His called out.
> **(Robert B. Callahan, Sr.)**

How foolish it is to wish to measure God's immensity by our measure. **(John Calvin)**

There is something else to realize about the struggles we face. "This is God's battle, we are given the privilege of being in it and of fighting as individual soldiers, but God's honor is involved in it all . . . His glory, and His honor are involved at every point! Be strong in the Lord, remember that He is there and it is His. Further, the whole movement of salvation is for God's glory; not simply for our deliverance, but for God's glory primarily." **(Martyn Lloyd-Jones)**

My goal is God Himself, not joy, nor peace, but Himself my God. **(Author Unknown)**

There is no ultimate knowledge of God apart from the Lord Jesus Christ and the full and the perfect revelation that is in Him. **(Martyn Lloyd-Jones)**

When once the concentration is on God, all the margins of life are free and under the dominance of God alone. There is no responsibility on you for the work; the only responsibility you have is to keep in living constant touch with God, and to see that you allow nothing to hinder your cooperation with Him. But, be careful to remember one thing only: To be absolutely devoted to your co-worker. **(Oswald Chambers)**

Calvin eloquently describes this special way saying, God "is cheated of His glory if we think that the Gospel is given to us either by chance, or by the will or activity of men." **(John Calvin)**

There is no teaching so harmful or adverse to our souls, to a right relationship with God, than the universal Fatherhood of God, and that Jesus did not need to come into the world to shed His blood, die on the Cross, and atone for our sins and sinfulness. **(Robert B. Callahan, Sr.)**

God forbid that I should glory save in the Cross of our Lord Jesus Christ. **(Robert B. Callahan, Sr.)**

We fail to recognize God in that we are not willing to accept that he is good to us. We fail to recognize ourselves in that we are not to accept (the truth) that we should submit ourselves to Him. **(Otto Weber)**

Everyone who knows and is persuaded that he is chastised by God ought at once to advance to the realization that it happens because he is loved by God. **(John Calvin)**

Human relationships do not come first: they never come first in the Bible, it is always man's relationship to God first. **(Martyn Lloyd Jones)**

To know God and to have fellowship with God means of necessity truth and truthfulness. (**Martyn Lloyd-Jones**)

The renowned theologian, John Calvin, expounds upon the phrase *giving thanks always* saying, that this is a pleasure which ought never to bore us by custom; an exercise of which we ought never to weary. The innumerable benefits which we receive from God yield fresh cause of joy and thanksgiving. At the same time, he warns believers, that it will be ungodly and disgraceful laziness, if they shall not all through their life study and practice the praises of God. (**John Calvin**)

11

GOD'S CHILDREN

There is no such thing as a mere, mortal Christian. (**C.S. Lewis**)

When we are members of the body of Christ we are children of God, therefore, we are to conduct ourselves as His children. We are to put on the new man in truth and He is to govern our conduct and our activities. Remember, when we do this people are going to judge God, judge the Gospel, judge Christ by what they see in us. It is an awesome thought! Of course people are wrong to judge in that manner, but they do, and you cannot do anything about it. (**Robert B. Callahan, Sr.**)

What happens when we "*walk as children of light?*"

There is fruit and it is evident in goodness, righteousness, and truth.

There are certain innate characteristics about fruit. It does not appear over night. It is not stamped out, or fabricated, or ready made.

What about fruit trees?

> Did you ever notice that at first they are barren, then they get buds and flowers, then the fruit is pollinated, it receives light.
> You will note that there are some things within the fruit tree that develop or I should say respond to the light and then something needs to make them fertile, then the fruit begins to appear, it grows, develops, and matures.

> It does not happen suddenly, it takes time, nutrients, care, pruning, spraying and picking. There is no such thing as instant fruit, nor are there instant Christians, nor immediate mature members of Christ's body. **(Robert B. Callahan, Sr.)**

We are all members of Christ's body, though we may have different assignments and callings. There is no division between the priesthood and laity. That is a development, which occurred within the Roman Church and has been perpetuated through the ages and the different denominations. **(Robert B. Callahan, Sr.)**

If we are children of God, we ought to be imitators of Him. **(John Calvin)**

Since in Christ we are a fruitful vine, out of Christ what are we but withered little branches. **(St. Augustine)**

When people accept Christ, they become new creatures. They may say they are going to change and conform to the teachings contained in Scripture, yet they are going to do it under their own power. It can not be done! No, it cannot be done! It can be done only through God's power. **(Robert B. Callahan, Sr.)**

A goodly portion of our lives is lived in the realm of experiences, feelings, sensations, sensibilities, desires, moods, and states. This is more elemental than the mind, and we should always be struggling to attain a mastery over it by using the mind and the understanding. **(Martyn Lloyd-Jones)**

If a person does not accept and believe in the grace of God, the person and work of the Lord Jesus Christ, and the power of the Holy Spirit, then that person is not in Christ. **(Robert B. Callahan, Sr.)**

We are the children of Israel. We are members of Christ's body. We are to *"be strong in the Lord."* We are to know what Scripture says and God requires. We are to know the Lord Jesus Christ better than we know any person.

Not just the miracles He performs, not just His words, sayings and the commands He gives, not just His actions and His obedience, but Him as the Son of God, Him as God-Man, Him as the Saviour, Him as friend and defender, and Him as our companion on life's journey. **(Robert B. Callahan, Sr.)**

What we are considering in these four verses (Eph. 1:11–14) was intended for Christians, not non-Christians. These verses contain truths for the children of God, for those who have received the Holy Spirit, have had their minds enlightened, and have achieved some understanding.

This teaching, this illumination, is not for the natural man who really does not understand salvation, and who gets himself in the way of God's call and God's message. **(Robert B. Callahan, Sr.)**

Paul points out that we are not to pride ourselves on what we were, what we are, and on what we are becoming. We are not to boast about our accomplishments. We are to recognize that there are two kinds of assurance: The first rests on the promises of God, so that the believer is convinced in his heart that God will never leave him, and relying on this unconquerable conviction he stands up to Satan and sin, cheerful and undaunted. At the same time, however, remembering his own weakness, he falls back on God in fear and humility, and in his anxiety willingly commits himself to Him. This kind of assurance is a holy thing, and cannot be separated from faith. **(John Calvin)**

We make room for Christ's grace when with a resigned mind we feel and confess our own weakness. **(John Calvin)**

There is nothing in Scripture which may not contribute to your instruction and the training of your life. **(John Calvin)**

Many people feel that once they accept Christ they will have a life of relative ease, that problems and difficulties will evaporate, as though, "there will be no fight, there will be no struggle, effort will not be required. So when they find that, on the contrary, they have grave difficulties and [are in] a mighty battle they are utterly discouraged." **(Martyn Lloyd-Jones)**

The Lord Jesus came to give us salvation. This ultimately means that we know God. Real Christianity is to know God. **(Robert B. Callahan, Sr.)**

The Christian is a man who sees life steadily and he sees it whole, and therefore he is not erratic. **(Matthew Arnold)**

A sense of wonder, amazement, and surprise. In other words, the true Christian does not say, 'Of course I am saved.' He says, it is an amazing thing that I should be saved at all. How did the almighty God ever bring Himself to look upon me? **(Martyn Lloyd-Jones)**

We have Christian attributes and experience, but we do not abandon ourselves to Christ, we do not commit fully and completely to Him. When we get into difficult circumstances, we impoverish His ministry by saying, "of course He cannot do anything," and we struggle down into the deeps and try to get the water for ourselves. Beware of the satisfaction of sinking back and saying, It can not be done. However, you know it can be done if you look to Jesus. **(Oswald Chambers)**

Our conversation is to be used for the upbuilding of the Body of Christ. **(Ruth Paxson)**

I confess that I do not know, that I cannot understand. I become 'as a little child,' and I look up into the face of Him who is the Way, the Truth, and the Life! But from the moment you enter it in that way you begin to use your understanding, and it grows and develops, and there is literally no end to it. **(Martyn Lloyd-Jones)**

No one is a believer who is not holy and no one is holy who is not a believer. **(Dr. William Temple)**

There are heart Christians and there are nominal Christians. The heart Christians know the Lord Jesus Christ. **(Gil Green)**

A Christian (is) to watch . . . that he may keep the Lord's charge and do the duty imposed upon him as a Christian. This is not a temporary duty, but for his whole lifetime. **(William Gurnall)**

We are to have full knowledge of God the Father. Think of what that means! It does not mean a superficial knowledge or a self-generated knowledge, but a scripturally based knowledge as revealed to us by the Holy Spirit. It is not served on a platter or with a spoon. It requires extra effort on our part. We are to pray, read, study, listen, and spend the necessary time to acquire full knowledge. **(Robert B. Callahan, Sr.)**

The godly calmly wait for Christ and do not dread His presence. **(John Calvin)**

Only the person who knows he is a child of God:
- has a complete view of life,
- knows this world leads to the next,
- knows the priorities of really living in this world,
- knows this is God's world,
- knows he must consider the world to which he is going,
- knows he should meditate *"on the riches of the glory of his inheritance in the saints."*

(Robert B. Callahan, Sr.)

The more I know, the more I shall be encouraged to forsake sin and to get ready for that which God has prepared for me. **(Robert B. Callahan, Sr.)**

When a person truly desires to be strong, he must not also refuse to be weak. **(John Calvin)**

The greatest saints have always testified to the fierceness of the battle, to their own weakness, to their own inability. **(Martyn Lloyd-Jones)**

Religious excitement originating by direct contact with God will always enlarge and exalt our conception of God's greatness, and will deepen our sense of dependence on Him . . . , but as emotion becomes more intense and as our conceptions of the Christian life become more and more glorious, the infinite greatness of God's righteousness and power and grace will inspire us with deeper wonder and awe.

On the other hand, religious excitement created by the imagination, though it may suggest lofty ideas of moral and spiritual perfection, and inspire a vehement and chivalrous desire to translate these ideas into conduct, will leave us with a new sense of our own greatness rather than a new sense of the greatness of God. (**R. W. Dale**)

A tiny spark of light led them to heaven, but now that the sun of righteousness shines on us what excuse shall we offer if we still hold to the earth or the things of the world? (**John Calvin**)

The failure to live the Christian life, or the life in Christ, ultimately results from the failure to understand the teachings of Scripture and the truth as it is found in Christ Jesus. If there is anger, malice, hatred, bitterness, or an unforgiving spirit, it is because we do not realize the Holy Spirit dwells within us and we grieve Him when we succumb to these temptations. That is Doctrine! We cannot go on being like that when we truly comprehend doctrine. (**Robert B. Callahan, Sr.**)

While living in the Pittsburgh area, we attended the First Presbyterian Church, which is located in the heart of the city. It was my privilege to usher in the balcony, where an elderly gentleman sat in the same pew every Sunday. He lived at the top of Mt. Washington which is across the Monongahela River from the city. The distance is approximately three to four miles. This gentleman walked that distance twice Sunday in all types of weather, even in the coldest winter months. One Sunday I said to him, "Why don't you take the street car?" He responded, "Bob, I do not have much money. By walking I can take the street car money and put it in the offering plate." He cast his mite in out of his want, with a joyful heart. (**Robert B. Callahan, Sr.**)

The saints are able bodied men, not by nature, nor by one act of ordination, (e.g. by their baptism), but only in as much as again and again they take up the special armor given to them. Whoever renders service, (shall do it) as one who renders it by the strength which God supplies . . . the armor, or strength, that is "put on" is equated with the "New Man" who is identified with Christ. (**Markus Barth**)

Believers particularly . . . cannot progress in the Gospel until first they have been humbled, and this cannot happen until they are aware of their sins. (**John Calvin**)

For this should be borne in mind . . . , for if they have defects mixed with their virtues, if they are persecuted out of hatred, if they are attacked with curses, these are not merely the rods of their heavenly instructor, but the buffetings which are designed to restrain all haughtiness and fill them with modesty. Therefore let all godly men take note. What a dreadful poison pride is, so that the only antidote to it is another poison. (**St. Augustine**)

There is nothing that (fosters) harmony better than this feeling for each other where each one realizes that he is enriched by the benefits of others every bit as much as they, and that when they suffer loss, he is impoverished along with them. (**John Calvin**)

Paul believed that the gospel was so wonderful that it was not possible for men to see its glory unless they were taught of God. Therefore, he told the followers at Ephesus that he continually prayed for God to give them a *"spirit of wisdom and revelation in the knowledge of him [that] the eyes of your understanding being enlightened, that ye may know what is the hope of his calling, and what [are] the riches of the glory of his inheritance in the saints."* (**Robert B. Callahan, Sr.**)

If we claim (profess) that we are church members (go to church) having fellowship with God, yet walk in darkness (according to the ways of the world), then we are liars in whom there is no truth. (**Martyn Lloyd-Jones**)

He openly declares that He does not pray for the world, for He is solicitous only for His own flock which He received from the Father's hand . . . Christ expressly declares that they who are given to Him belong to the Father. (**John Calvin**)

The Son of God, became the Son of Man, that the sons of men might become the sons of God. (**John Calvin**)

If the Lord aids us by His extraordinary power, we have no reason to be irresolute in battle. **(John Calvin)**

[Luther] suddenly saw that the monastic way was not God's way, and that was the beginning of the great Protestant Reformation. Thank God that that which Luther had to unlearn is not the Christian teaching, for the logical end of the monastic argument is that you cannot be a true Christian and still live in the world. **(Martyn Lloyd-Jones)**

It is important, though it may not be the most pleasant thing to hear, but niceness, friendliness, and sentimental notions of brotherliness do not constitute Christianity, or mean someone is a member of the Body of Christ. These qualities can be evident in people who are not members of the Body or who even deny it. However, you cannot have Christianity, or be members of the Body of Christ, without the truth, that is in Christ. **(Robert B. Callahan, Sr.)**

When we are babes, or children in Christ, we have the ability to express ourselves, but when we mature we have the ability to think about what Christ wants and what the word of God has to say to us. That is a significant difference. **(Robert B. Callahan, Sr.)**

When once the concentration is on God, all the margins of life are free and under the dominance of God alone. There is no responsibility on you for the work; the only responsibility you have is to keep in living constant touch with God, and to see that you allow nothing to hinder your cooperation with Him. But, be careful to remember one thing only. To be absolutely devoted to your co-worker. **(Oswald Chambers)**

No root of bitterness, no system of wrath, no trace of anger, no echo of clamor, no slime of evil speaking and no dregs of malice are to remain in a person, nor are they to be seen in one's conduct at any time or place. **(Ruth Paxson)**

The Christian teaching realizes that it cannot transform society as a whole; it must go on trusting that gradually the teaching will act as a leaven, and that men will become more and more enlightened. The time lag is not to be explained in terms of the failure of biblical teachings; it is to be explained in terms of the blindness of the world to Christian teaching. Christians have been given wisdom by God and the power to be patient and to wait until the right time for action has arrived. **(Martyn Lloyd-Jones)**

For this should be borne in mind . . ., if they have defects mixed with their virtues, if they are persecuted out of hatred, if they are attacked with curses, these are not merely the rods of their heavenly instructor, but the buffetings which are designed to restrain all haughtiness and fill them with modesty. Therefore let all godly men take note. What a dreadful poison pride is, so that the only antidote to it is another poison. **(St. Augustine)**

12

GOD'S LOVE

Brotherly love is a gift of God, not an achievement over which man exercises control . . . It indicates that the peace which God has created brings forth two things, "love" for thy neighbor and "faith" in God. (**Markus Barth**)

It is enough that Paul under the influence of the Holy Spirit says we are to endeavor with all lowliness, meekness, long suffering and forbearing to keep the unity of the Spirit in the bond of peace, but then he has the audacity or, if you will, the cool, calm, composure to say we are to do all this to one another in love. (**Robert B. Callahan, Sr.**)

Paul's design is to reduce all the precepts of the law to love, so that we may know we are duly obeying the commandments when we are maintaining love. (**John Calvin**)

A beautiful description of the husband's love for his wife was written by Chrysostom. He says, "Hast thou seen the measure of obedience? Hear also the measure of love. Wouldst thou that thy wife shouldst obey thee as the church doth Christ? Have care thyself for her as Christ for the Church. And if it be needful that thou shouldst give thy life for her, or be cut to pieces a thousand times, or endure anything whatever, refuse it not . . . He brought the Church to his feet by his great care, not by threats nor fear nor any such things; so do thou conduct thyself towards thy wife." (**Chrysostom**)

Whenever a person falls in love–that is, if he or she loves very deeply–there is always something in the life of the person loved that reaches out and elicits love. You simply do not fall in love by making up your mind that you are going to fall in love. There is always something about the person loved that calls forth love. And yet love is called forth in such a way as to do violence to our own will. We live freely. In fact, we are never so free as when we do the will of the person whom we love. But love can never be explained in terms of our own will. **(John Leith)**

Paul, under the influence of the Holy Spirit states that God, by His commandments, wanted to instruct us in the duty of love. Isn't that interesting? The duty of love!! Yes, love has its duties. **(Robert B. Callahan, Sr.)**

Love seeks the well being of everyone and the opportunity to do good or to benefit others. **(Robert B. Callahan, Sr.)**

There can be no genuine assurance before God unless His spirit produces in us the fruit of love. **(John Calvin)**

It may help your understanding and application of this Scripture to keep in mind the manner in which Christ and His Church submit themselves to each other which is the prime example for the husband and wife. Ruth Paxson says, "Christ submitted Himself in self-denying, self-sacrificing love, even, unto death, for His bride, whom he cherishes and cares for in the most tender manner. The Church, the Bride, responds with the submission of absolute loyalty in yieldedness and obedience. It is the mutual submission of a pure love for a perfect lover." **(Ruth Paxson)**

It is not a slavish obedience to every whim and fancy of unreasonableness and selfishness on the part of the husband, but the loving and joyous subjection of loyalty to love. For the one to whom she is united as 'one flesh' she will have only respect and reverence. **(Ruth Paxson)**

The word constrain points out that everyone who truly considers and ponders the wonderful love that Christ has shown us in His death, cannot but be bound to Him by the tightest chain so as to devote Himself to His service. It is the person who has Christ dwelling in the heart by faith. It is the person who has a personal relationship with Christ as friend, as

Saviour, as the Son of God. Pray God that He will bless us with a deep and abiding love. **(John Calvin)**

Everyone who knows and is persuaded that he is chastised by God ought at once to advance to this realization that it happens because he is loved by God. **(John Calvin)**

God's gift of His Son was an exercise of divine will and was made for one reason only, to express His love toward us. Love has its perfect expression among people in the person of the Lord Jesus Christ. It is beautifully expressed by Paul to the Ephesians: *And to know the love of Christ which passeth knowledge, that ye might be filled with all the fullness of God* [Eph. 3:19]. **(Robert B. Callahan, Sr.)**

God's love (agape) expresses the deep, constant love and interest of a perfect God toward entirely unworthy individuals and produces a reverential love in them toward God and a practical love toward one's neighbors. **(Robert B. Callahan, Sr.)**

The love of Christ is really determined by keeping His teachings and being obedient unto Him. This is a unique rule. **(Robert B. Callahan, Sr.)**

The end of all our knowledge should be to receive fully the knowledge of Christ's love. That is the end, the objective, and the purpose of all doctrine. **(Robert B. Callahan, Sr.)**

There is nothing so dishonoring to God, His Son, His Spirit, and His Word as a spirit of self-satisfaction, whereby people wish to remain babes *in Christ* and refuse to scale the heights to *receive fully* the love of Christ.**(Robert B. Callahan, Sr.)**

Only a deep love to God can stand up to the trials, stresses, strains and hazards of life. Belief alone is not enough. It is essential and can take us a long way, but when life's storms and tests come it is not enough. It is love alone that stands and withstands. **(Martyn Lloyd-Jones)**

We can know that Christ loved us and gave Himself for us. We can know the faithfulness of His love, . . . its tenderness, . . . its fellowship, . . . (and) its patience . . . as we company with Him in prayer and in the study of His Word. **Ruth Paxson**)

Paul's design is to reduce all the precepts of the law to love, so that we may know we are duly obeying the commandments when we are maintaining love. (**John Calvin**)

Love is the special fruit of the Spirit, it is also a sure symbol of regeneration. (**John Calvin**)

Shakespeare states it very appropriately in one of his sonnets.

> Love is not Love
> Which alters when it alteration finds,
> Or bends with the remover to remove:
>
> O, no! It is an ever fixed mark,
> That looks on tempests, and is
> never shaken. (**William Shakespeare**)

What should be the results of nourishing and cherishing?

> The individuals receiving these benefits, by grace, should grow, develop and prosper in the Lord.
>
> When a person is nourished and cherished they should realize they are under the watchful care of the One who is providing for them.
>
> Unfortunately, many of us do not truly realize our Lord's great concern for us individually as well as collectively. (**Robert B. Callahan, Sr.**)

The issue is not what men did to the Lord Jesus Christ, but what God did to Him. That is the supreme issue. God gave His only begotten Son, Christ gave Himself up.

> Why? Because they both love us and it was the only way to provide for our salvation and to bring us into a right relationship with God. Their love is tough, strong, resilient, elastic, obedient, self-denying and forgiving. Further, their love fully and completely exemplifies the duties encompassed in their love. (**Robert B. Callahan, Sr.**)

If we really love Jesus then we will keep His commandments. People have many diverse thoughts and opinions about love. This is especially true about the love of Christ. However, true love of Christ is really determined by keeping His teachings and being obedient unto Him. This is the unique rule. However, we should realize that our affections and our emotions can be sinful and our love for Christ can be at fault unless it exhibits and expresses true and pure obedience to Him. Thy will be done! However, we cannot show pure obedience unless we know Him, His teachings and the truth that is in Him. **(Robert B. Callahan, Sr.)**

God loves the obedient, not the caviling *(irritating complaints and criticism.)* **(Martin Luther)**

Everyone who knows and is persuaded that he is chastised by God ought at once to advance to this realization that it happens because he is loved by God. This is difficult to accept and to realize. However, as Calvin further notes, "When believers find God in the midst of their punishments, they have a sure pledge of His loving kindness and his concern for their salvation." **(John Calvin)**

However severe and wrathful a judge God shows Himself to be towards unbelievers (and believers) whenever He punishes them, His primary purpose is to provide counsel for their salvation and to have them come into a right relationship with Himself. This is one way by which He demonstrates His fatherly love. **(John Calvin)**

God's nature is to love man. The Apostle John simply means, that God is the fountain of love. That this affection flows from God and is poured out where there is knowledge of Him. John is not speaking here of the essence of God, but is declaring what we experience Him to be. **(John Calvin)**

Everyone who knows and is persuaded that he is chastised by God ought at once to advance to this realization that it happens because he is loved by God. **(Robert B. Callahan, Sr.)**

When we are cornered, or troubled, the Lord opens a way; when we are oppressed or perplexed He comes to our aid; when we are surrounded he strengthens and supports us; when we are in deep trouble He will support us and stay with us. He will not allow us to be destroyed or overwhelmed. **(Robert B. Callahan, Sr.)**

God, the Father, loves us as He loved His Son. This is a staggering thought and statement. **(Robert B. Callahan, Sr.)**

"Thou Hidden Love of God"

Thou hidden love of God, whose height,
Whose depth unfathomed, no man knows,
I see from afar thy beauteous light,
Inwardly I sigh for thy repose;
My heart is pained, nor can it be
At rest until it finds rest in thee.

Tis mercy all, that thou has brought
My mind to seek her peace in thee;
Yet, while I seek but find thee not,
No peace my wandering soul shall see;
O when shall all my wanderings end,
And all my steps to thee-ward tend.
(Gerhard Tersteegen)

So in those bright pleasant moments when we think of the glory, wonder and perfection of what is waiting for us, and in those moments of despair when we suffer from doubts, unworthiness, hopelessness, we need to remember that the God who is working within us will keep us and prepare us for the glory that awaits us. Therefore, I can say with the Apostle Paul:

"I am persuaded, that neither death, nor life, nor angels, nor principalities, nor powers, nor things present, nor things to come, Nor height, nor depth, nor any other creature, shall be able to separate us from the love of God, which is Christ Jesus our Lord. **[Romans 8:38–39]**

13

GOD'S POWER

Paul is not, I repeat, is not praying that the Ephesians may realize their need for power and then ask God for it. But, He is praying that the Ephesian followers may realize that this power is in them. This is an important distinction. Further, the point of view, that a Christian has lived for years without the power of God and suddenly realizes his or her need for it and obtains it is just not scriptural. A person cannot be a Christian even for a moment if God's power does not sustain him. It is a fallacy to even think that God creates a new person and then leaves him alone for a day let alone for 40 or 50 years. Then, the person realizes his need for power and asks for it. When God puts his hand on someone He begins to exert His power and continues to do so. **(Robert B. Callahan, Sr.)**

When people accept Christ, they become new creatures. They may say they are going to change and conform to the teachings contained in Scripture, yet they are going to do it under their own power. It cannot be done! No, it cannot be done! It can be done only through God's power. **(Robert B. Callahan, Sr.)**

Suppose there is a well of fathomless trouble inside your heart, and Jesus comes and says—"Let not your heart be troubled". and you shrug your shoulders and say, "But, Lord the well is deep; You cannot draw up quietness and comfort out of it." No (He won't) He will bring them down from above. Jesus does not bring anything up from the well of human nature, or from earthen vessels. **(Oswald Chambers)**

Remember, He has the power! The New Testament teaching is rather explicit. If we are commanded to do something, then we should proceed with full confidence that the Lord has the power to do it and the will to do it. Why? Because we are members of His body and we are *in Christ*. **(Robert B. Callahan, Sr.)**

He exhorts them to courage, but then reminds them to ask from God a supply of what in themselves they lack; and at the same time promise that, if they ask for it, the power of God will be displayed. **(John Calvin)**

Hope is a supernatural grace of God, whereby the believer, through Christ expects and waits for all those good things of the promise, which at present he hath not received, or not fully. **(William Gurnall)**

One of the greatest failures of those who are *in Christ*, of those who are professing Christians, of those who attend worship services, is that all of us put a limit on God and His power. **(Robert B. Callahan, Sr.)**

O' but what truths are contained in the 2nd and 3rd verses of Onward, Christian Soldiers by Sabine Baring-Gould. The words state clearly what we have been studying in Ephesians and the New Testament. Listen to them:

> Like a mighty army moves the church of God.
> Brothers we are treading where the saints have trod.
> We are not divided, all one body we,
> One in hope and doctrine, one in charity.
>
> Crowns and thorns may perish, kingdoms rise and wane,
> But the church of Jesus, Constant will remain.
> Gates of hell can never 'Gainst that Church prevail;
> We have Christ's own promise, And that cannot fail.

Yet, the uninformed removed this magnificent, truthful hymn from our hymnals. What a travesty!" **(Robert B. Callahan, Sr.)**

Nicodemus thought a new life would be incredible. Christ tries to teach him that even in his bodily life, and ours, that the marvelous power of God is hidden. "If in this frail and transitory life God acts so powerfully ..., how absurd it is to want to measure by the apprehension of our own mind His secret work in the heavenly and supernatural life and believe no more than we can see!" **(John Calvin)**

He removes unfruitful branches, so they can be thrown into the fire and burned. He gets rid of them. **(John Calvin)**

Paul prays fervently for the ability of power within us and to know it is there. Some authorities say this petition refers to our future resurrection and that God's power will raise us from the dead. Since we are heirs and will receive our inheritance. However, it is more than that. In addition, and a very important addition, it refers to the whole of our Christian life–from beginning to end. God wants us to enjoy and use this power every day, every year. Any other interpretation is just ludicrous! God does not say or act on the basis that sometime in the future I'll show you my power. He does it now. **(Robert B. Callahan, Sr.)**

Why should we *"be strong in the Lord, and in the power of His might?"*

Probably the best explanation is provided by Calvin who said, "If the Lord aids us by His extraordinary power, we have no reason to be irresolute in battle." He exhorts them [the faithful] to courage, but then reminds them to ask from God a supply of what in themselves they lack; and at the same time promise that, if they ask for it, the power of God will be displayed. **(John Calvin)**

May we ask for what we lack? Think of what that means. We have to acknowledge our weaknesses, our insufficiencies, and our needs. That can be very difficult to do, yet we are to be confident that God will provide His power. **(Robert B. Callahan, Sr.)**

The cure for self-centeredness, self-pity, introspection, morbidity and similar afflictions is to know the glory and purpose of God. **(Robert B. Callahan, Sr.)**

Bearing all these teachings and truths in mind, my brethren, become strengthened and powerful inwardly in the Lord, and in the complete, perfect power of His strength which He bestows upon believers. **(Robert B. Callahan, Sr.)**

We make room for Christ's grace when with a resigned mind we feel and confess our own weakness. **(John Calvin)**

This almighty power of God is engaged for its (or our) defense; so as to bear up in the midst of all trials and temptations. Undauntedly, leaning on the arm of God almighty, as if it were his own strength. **(William Gurnall)**

> Unto him
> That is able to do
> all that we ask or think
> above all that we ask or think
> abundantly above all that we ask or think
> Exceeding abundantly above all that we ask or think
> According to the power that worketh in us.
> **(Ruth Paxson)**

Some (of the disciples) hesitated at first until Christ approached them nearer and more intimately. When they knew him in truth and certainty, then they worshipped Him . . . There is no doubt that his approach to them took away all doubts. Before relating that the office of teaching was laid upon them, Matthew says that Christ spoke first of His power, and rightly so . . . The Apostles would never be persuaded to undertake such a task of difficulty unless they knew that their Champion sat in heaven, and that supreme power was given to him. **(John Calvin)**

If the Lord aids us by His extraordinary power, we have no reason to be irresolute in battle. **(John Calvin)**

14

GOD'S PROVIDENCE

That even the greatest geniuses are like a traveler passing through a field at night who in a momentary lightning flash sees far and wide, but the sight vanishes so swiftly that he is plunged again into the darkness of the night before he can take even a step–let alone be directed on his way by its help. **(John Calvin)**

Arnold Toynbee, the renowned historian, said that the whole process of history, in a sense, is a matter of cycles. There is a rise, then a fall. There are ups and downs. A nation comes to power, stimulates others, then decay and decline set in and the powers fall. Then, the process repeats itself. **(Arnold Toynbee)**

The greatest triumph, which God ever won, was when Christ, after subduing sin, conquering death, and putting Satan to flight rose majestically to heaven, that He might exercise His glorious reign over the church. **(John Calvin)**

Luther suddenly saw that the monastic way was not God's way, and that was the beginning of the great Protestant Reformation. Thank God that that which Luther had to unlearn is not the Christian teaching, for the logical end of the monastic argument is that you cannot be a true Christian and still live in the world. **(Martyn Lloyd-Jones)**

Patiently God, through our history, accommodates his ways of revelation to our condition. Thus, par excellence, the Word made flesh and the written Word from which he speaks is God accommodating himself to us. **(Ford Lewis Battles)**

Hope is a supernatural grace of God, whereby the believer, through Christ, expects and waits for all those good things of the promise, which at present he hath not received, or not fully. **(William Gurnall)**

15

GOD'S TRUTH

The truth, the highest truth, we are to know is in Jesus. The truth is in Him. The truth cannot be known if it is separated from Him. This truth is what the Apostle taught the Ephesians and what he teaches us. (**R.W. Dale**)

As the Apostle Paul abundantly demonstrates when a minister or teacher effectively presents "the truth" as it is found in Jesus Christ and effectively discharges his duties, then there is no room for evasion or ignoring the teaching on the part of the hearers. (**Robert B. Callahan, Sr.**)

The revelation of Christ in truth must result in the realization of Christ in life. (**Ruth Paxson**)

We fail to recognize God in that we are not willing to accept that he is good to us. We fail to recognize ourselves in that we are not willing to accept [the truth] that we should submit ourselves to him. (**Otto Weber**)

To know God and to have fellowship with God means of necessity, truth and truthfulness. (**Martyn Lloyd-Jones**)

Jesus said, *"But he that doeth the truth cometh to the light."* [John 3:21] Augustine expounds upon this by saying, 'That he that 'doeth the truth' acknowledges how wretched we are and destitute of all well-doing. (**St. Augustine**)

If religious truth does not meet the just demands of the intellect as well as of the moral nature, it will be regarded with languid interest and will at last be either silently abandoned or rejected with open hostility and scorn. **(R.W. Dale)**

We cannot completely and fully understand all the truths of God as we begin and proceed on our journey of faith. God's truths are revealed to us along the way, as we are able to grasp and understand them. We are not fully capable of understanding all that God knows, but we are capable of increasing in faith and wisdom. **(Robert B. Callahan, Sr.)**

The purpose of the doctrine (truth) . . . and the knowledge we have been acquiring is one and the same. It is to bring us to the foot of the Cross. It is to bring us to our Lord and Saviour Jesus Christ. It is to bring us into a personal relationship with the Son of God. **(Robert B. Callahan, Sr.)**

To tell people that what a man believes does not matter as long as he lives a good life and does good is not only a denial of the gospel, it is bound to discourage people from believing the only truth which can save them. **(Martyn Lloyd-Jones)**

The truth as it is used by Paul, is the objective truth which I possess in a subjective manner. **(Martyn Lloyd-Jones)**

Truth is a pure and right knowledge of God, and Jesus Christ is that Truth providing knowledge of God. **(Robert B. Callahan, Sr.)**

The next thing it is not, is that a person's life is more important than what he or she believes. People may say that a certain person is not a Christian, but their good deeds prove they are. Balderdash! What a person believes does make a difference. To tell people that what a man believes does not matter as long as he lives a good life and does good is not only a denial of the gospel, it is bound to discourage people from believing the only truth which can save them. **(Martyn Lloyd-Jones)**

When learning Christ, we will grow in Christ, we will be in Christ, we will walk in Christ, and we will realize the truth in Christ. We are to hear and accept the fact that *the truth is in Jesus*, then we are to live, act, and speak according to the standard as it is found in the Lord Jesus Christ. There can be no compromises, no divided interests. As Scripture says, Ye were, Ye are, Become ye. The power comes from God. It is through this power that we learn Christ and are changed. (**Robert B. Callahan, Sr.**)

Christ expressly says that the truth by which God sanctifies His sons exists no where but in the word. (**John Calvin**)

If we are to live our lives according to the Word of Truth, we are to know the teachings contained in Scripture. It is not a case of feelings or philosophy. It is a case of doctrine and truth. (**Robert B. Callahan, Sr.**)

Probably the greatest irony, or incongruity perpetrated by the Church at large in the 20th Century or early 21st is that you can have the morality or ethics or, as I prefer the righteousness of the Bible, without "the whole counsel of God," or the truth as it is revealed in Christ Jesus. You cannot construct a multi-story building without a foundation. There is only one foundation! The truth as it is found in Christ. (**Author Unknown**)

16

GRACE

Man's reconciliation by God's grace is inseparable from God's confidence and command that man be reconciled. (**Markus Barth**)

Paul's commitment to Christ and his dependence upon Him is such that he proclaims the gospel and applies it to those institutions that have been considered secular. Paul praises Christ in such a way that neither sin, nor death, nor former divisions, nor institutions, nor structures, and certainly not marriage, can escape the power and riches of grace. (**Markus Barth**)

When a person is exposed to the light or receives it as a gift, then he or she is exposed to the creative, redemptive, life-giving God–not just with a better self. (**Markus Barth**)

No one except the Messiah can and will establish it among his people . . . it is a gift of God! (**Markus Barth**)

Patiently God, through our history, accommodates his ways of revelation to our condition. Thus, par excellence, the Word made flesh and the written Word from which he speaks is God accommodating himself to us. (**Ford Lewis Battles**)

The establishment of the right relationship between a person and God is by the grace of God. (**Robert B. Callahan, Sr.**)

Therefore, it seems the Apostle is saying that the Riches of God's grace have provided us with forgiveness and its many benefits, and that His grace gives us the wisdom and prudence necessary to obtain a real knowledge of the mystery of God's will and His eternal purpose in Christ Jesus. (**Robert B. Callahan, Sr.**)

God's grace abounds. It is poured out on me. It is wisdom that not only gives understanding, but includes my affections, my love, my interest and all of me. (**Robert B. Callahan, Sr.**)

When we are joined to Christ, we are no longer under the law, but under grace. This does not mean we no longer have to keep God's commands, but it means our relationship to God has changed; it is no longer a legal one. Instead, it is a personal one due to the grace of God. (**Robert B. Callahan, Sr.**)

Paul knew himself. he had been the chief sinner. He had been a Pharisee, proud, self-satisfied, contented, self-righteous, and boastful. It was then when he deserved anything but God's grace, that is what he received: God's Abundant Grace! (**Robert B. Callahan, Sr.**)

He (Christ) openly declares that He does not pray for the world, for He is solicitous only for His own flock which He received from the Father's hand. Christ expressly declares that they who are given to Him belong to the Father. (**John Calvin**)

Paul means that we, who are unholy by nature, are born again by His spirit into holiness, so that we may serve God. From this we gather, as Calvin says, that we cannot be justified freely by faith alone, if we do not at the same time live in holiness. For those two gifts of grace are inseparable, they are tied together by a firm tight bond and if anyone tries to separate them or pull them apart, then he is in a sense trying to tear Christ to pieces. (**Robert B. Callahan, Sr.**)

There is one very important point to recognize and believe completely, no matter how much of the fullness of Christ we enjoy or experience today, there is always more fullness tomorrow. Every tomorrow can bring ever-greater fullness. (**Robert B. Callahan, Sr.**)

For Christ washes us, not that we may return to rolling in our pollution, but that we may retain through our life the purity which we have once received. **(John Calvin)**

Evil deeds are given the punishment they deserve, but in rewarding good deeds, God does not have regard to their merit or worth. No work of ours is so full and complete in all its parts as to deserve God's approval. **(John Calvin)**

Suppose there is a well of fathomless trouble inside your heart, and Jesus comes and says–Let not your heart be troubled; and you shrug your shoulders and say, "But, Lord the well is deep; You cannot draw up quietness and comfort out of it." No, He will bring them down from above. Jesus does not bring anything up from the well of human nature. **(Oswald Chambers)**

There is a gulf between us and God that is revealed in the law. There is only one way it can be bridged. The law can be fulfilled only through the grace that is in and through Jesus Christ. Also, the reality of the "image of God" is revealed through Him. Jesus is the man for God, out of God, and before God. It is in the Lord Jesus Christ that our rejection is terminated in, through and upon Him. In this manner our judgment is set aside by God's grace. A peculiarity of this is that only in and through Him does our real rejection come to light. Who we are by nature, our sinful condition, to whom the law has been given and the total inability to keep it. These things cannot be recognized outside the reality of Jesus Christ and Him crucified. **(Robert B. Callahan, Sr.)**

If we wish to be Christ's (accept and follow Him), we must be regenerate by God, but this is no ordinary gift. **(John Calvin)**

You have inherited the Divine nature, says Peter, now screw your attention down and form habits, give diligence, concentrate. "Add" means all that character means. No man is born either naturally or supernaturally with character, he has to make character. Nor are we born with habits; we have to form habits on the basis of the new life God has put into us . . . Drudgery is the touchstone of character. The great hindrance in spiritual life is that we will look for big things to do . . . . *Jesus took a towel . . . and began to wash the disciples feet.*

There are times when there is no illumination and no thrill, but just the daily round, the common task. Routine is God's way of saving us between our times of inspiration. Do not expect God always to give you His thrilling minutes, but learn to live in the domain of drudgery by the power of God.

It is the "adding" that is difficult. We say we do not expect God to carry us to heaven on flowery beds of ease, and yet we act as if we did! The tiniest detail in which I obey has all the omnipotent power of the grace of God behind it. If I do my duty, not for duty's sake, but because I believe God is engineering my circumstances, then at the very point of my obedience the whole super grace of God is mine through the Atonement." **(Oswald Chambers)**

These verses [Eph. 4:22–24] are the crossroads between God's sovereign work through grace and man's cooperative action through faith. **(Ruth Paxson)**

We saints that have habitual grace, yet this lies like water at the bottom of a well, which will not ascend with all our pumping till God pour in his exciting grace, and then it comes. To will is more than to think, to exert our will into action more than both. These are of God: *"It is God which worketh in you both to will and to do of his good pleasure."* **[Phil. 2:3] (William Gurnall)**

There is a point in grace as much above the ordinary Christian as the ordinary Christian is above the worldling. **(Charles Spurgeon)**

Paul does not teach here what men are capable of by their natural powers, but what the Lord does through them by His grace. He, by Himself, acts through them in such a way that they, in turn, work with Him for a common end. **(John Calvin)**

We make room for God's Grace when with a resigned mind we feel and confess our own weakness. **(John Calvin)**

And can it be that I should gain an interest in the Saviour's blood? Died He for me, who caused His pain? For me, who Him to death pursued. Amazing love! How can it be, that thou, my God, should die for me.
(Charles Wesley)

It may help us to consider the words of John Newton who wrote the wonderful hymn Amazing Grace–How Sweet the Sound. He also penned the following verse:

>Thou art coming to King,
>Large petitions with thee bring;
>For this grace and power are such,
>None can ever ask too much.
>**(John Calvin)**

"Come We that Love the Lord"

>The men of grace have found,
>Glory begun below,
>Celestial fruit on earthly ground,
>From faith and hope may grow.
>
>The hill of Zion yields,
>A thousand Sacred Sweets,
>Before we reach the heavenly fields,
>Or walk the golden streets.
>
>There shall we see His face,
>and never, never sin,
>There from the rivers of His Grace,
>Drink endless pleasures in.
>
>Then let our songs abound,
>and every tear be dry,
>We're marching through Immanuel's ground,
>To fairer worlds on high.
>**(Isaac Watts)**

17

HOLINESS

There is an interesting anecdote to share with you: A man once said when discussing miracles that when the church could say, "Silver and gold have I none, it could say in the name of Jesus Christ, of Nazareth, rise up and walk. Today the church has silver and gold, it has become large and powerful, it has lobbyists, but it seems to have forgotten holiness". (**Author Unknown**)

Had man kept his primitive righteousness, Christ's pain and pains would have been spared. It was because of man's lost holiness that he came to recover . . . both God and man, between whom Christ comes to negotiate, call for holiness. God's glory and man's happiness; neither of which can be attained except holiness be restored to man. (**William Gurnall**)

The godly calmly wait for Christ and do not dread His presence. (**John Calvin**)

It is a definite sign of our union with God when we are conformed to Him. However, let us make one point clear it is not the purity of our daily living that reconciles us to God. It means that when God's purity shines in us that our unity with him is assured. Of course, it must be stated and acknowledged that whenever God's holiness fills us there is no room for filth, uncleanness and darkness. We cannot live properly unless we cleave to God. Our fellowship is to be with God, not just with one another. (**Robert B. Callahan, Sr.**)

To put on Christ means here to be defended on every side by the power of His Spirit, and thus rendered fit to discharge all the duties of holiness. **(John Calvin)**

Those "who do not appreciate this truth being chosen to holiness and show some signs of holiness in their lives, are not chosen, are not Christians." **(Martyn Lloyd-Jones)**

No one is a believer who is not holy and no one is holy who is not a believer. **(Dr. William Temple)**

The image of God in holiness and righteousness is reborn in us on the condition of our sharing in eternal life and glory. **(John Calvin)**

18

HOLY COMMUNION

The cup of blessing is communion through the blood of Christ. It means that the believers are bound together by the blood of Christ. For what reason? So that they might become one Body. This kind of unity is properly called communion. **(Robert B. Callahan, Sr.)**

It is by the *"cup of blessing"* or by the blood of Christ that we are grafted into His body. It is by this means that He lives in us and we live in Him. **(Robert B. Callahan, Sr.)**

You are well aware of the power of the Holy Supper, for in it we are ingrafted into the Body of the Lord. **(John Calvin)**

When we partake of the Lords Supper, we are in the presence of our Lord Jesus Christ, He is in our midst. We meet Him with all our deficiencies, frailties, and weaknesses. We are to obey the command, *This do in remembrance of me.* [Luke 22:19b] This command does not mean "in memory of." It does mean an affectionate call to obey the Lord Jesus Christ. **(Robert B. Callahan, Sr.)**

What is the Lord's Supper? It is to be understood and accepted as: a divine moment; the real presence of our risen, glorified Lord; a meeting place appointed and promised by Christ for His own followers, the members of His own body; and a thanksgiving for our redemption! In addition, it proclaims the Cross of Christ, His broken body, His shed blood; and it points to the final consummation and reunion with Christ. Therefore, how can we do anything but give thanks for all things unto God the Father, in the name our Lord Jesus Christ. **(Robert B. Callahan, Sr.)**

There needs to be an awakening of our minds to the presence of Christ, to the reality of being members of His body, to confessing our sins, to the need of forgiveness, and to accepting with humility and confidence His forgiveness of our sins. **(Robert B. Callahan, Sr.)**

The bread is the promise He will be there. The cup is the promise that He is the Saviour who initiated the new covenant by His death. **(Robert B. Callahan, Sr.)**

19

HOLY SPIRIT

The Holy Spirit may be lesser known than God, the Father and the Lord Jesus Christ, but He is a divine Member of the Holy Trinity. May the following designations illuminate the Holy Spirit's traits as you continue Walking With Jesus.

A) PERSON

Whatever can be said about faith, repentance, redemption, the Christian life, justification, and even the sacraments involves the Spirit. Wherever you turn with respect to God and to Jesus Christ you find the Holy Spirit. **(Robert B. Callahan, Sr.)**

Nowhere in the scripture is the Holy Spirit described as the Word of God. That description is confined solely to our Lord Jesus Himself. The Holy Spirit is not the Word. **(Martyn Lloyd-Jones)**

The Holy Spirit is God personally at work in the world . . . The Holy Spirit is God personally at work to inspire, to make alive, to convince, to enable Christians to speak and act as Christians. The Holy Spirit unites us with Jesus Christ and his work for us and our salvation. It is not enough to know Jesus Christ and his work for us and our salvation. It is not enough to know Jesus Christ as an objective historical fact, to know what Jesus Christ is for us, unless we also know that Jesus Christ is in us, not substantially, but in a personal union. **(John Leith)**

The Holy Spirit is a person that is why we can grieve Him. You cannot grieve an influence, or a power, or a principle, or a thing. But you can grieve a person. We can grieve the Holy Spirit. **(Robert B. Callahan, Sr.)**

It is clear . . . that the grace of the Spirit is a striking testimony to His divinity. **(John Calvin)**

B) FUNCTION

Man needs two things. He needs the ability to see and he needs the power and strength to use his spiritual abilities and faculties. It is the Holy Spirit that provides these needs. **(Robert B. Callahan, Sr.)**

Jesus says *the Spirit of truth*. [John 14:17] Christ is saying that the Holy Spirit is the teacher of truth. We are to be taught inwardly by Him otherwise our minds are held captive by vanity and falsehood.

In these verses Jesus exhorts His disciples not to be puffed up, not to rely on their pride and reason for they cannot know Him if the Holy Spirit does not operate within them and fill them. John Calvin says, "Christ's words show that nothing relating to the Holy Spirit can be learned from human reason, but that He is known only by the experience in faith."

We know Him because the Spirit dwells within us. If the Spirit does not dwell within us, then we will not know Him. **(Robert B. Callahan, Sr.)**

It is the peculiar function of the Holy Spirit to bring us to a knowledge of God. But without the Holy Spirit full knowledge of God is impossible. **(Robert B. Callahan, Sr.)**

The renowned theologian B. B. Warfield clarifies this truth (sealed with the Holy Spirit) regarding both the Jewish Christians of that day and the Gentile Christians saying, "that Christians have been sealed by the Holy Spirit unto the day of redemption, (and that we) should consider the nature of strength of the motive thence arising to us, who are the recipients of His (sealing), to refrain from the sin which grieves Him, and to seek the life of holiness which pleases Him." **(B. B. Warfield)**

The Holy Spirit reveals to us the exceeding great and precious promises of God in Christ. As He does, we begin to realize that God is the Father of Jesus Christ and He is our Father. (**Robert B. Callahan, Sr.**)

The new person (in Christ) will be renewed daily in the Spirit of his or her mind by the Holy Spirit. He will always be with them and never cease to help them. Thank God. (**Robert B. Callahan, Sr.**)

C) PURPOSE

The guarantee of true unity in the church of believers is the unity of the Holy Spirit. The outpouring of the Holy Spirit is essential, it is a prerequisite. It alone can bring about the unity of holiness, the unity of a holy people, when holiness is the main characteristic then the unity takes care of itself. (**Robert B. Callahan, Sr.**)

The Holy Spirit is in you. God takes up His abode in you . . . We are not left to ourselves. (**Martyn Lloyd-Jones**)

What is needed is the Spirit opening the Word, and opening my mind and opening my heart. (**Martyn Lloyd-Jones**)

There is not a text in the whole New Testament which says that this blessing of the power and of the fire of the Spirit is to be confined only to certain people to exceptional saints, or preachers or someone whom God wants to use in a special manner. No, it is *"to you, and your children, and to as many as are afar off."* [**Acts 2:30**] (**Martyn Lloyd-Jones**)

Increasing in faith and knowledge cannot be accomplished without the Holy Ghost filling us, without hearing and learning the truth as it is in Jesus. (**Robert B. Callahan, Sr.**)

The Holy Spirit causes us to realize something of the truth concerning God's holiness. We really do not know much about this until the Holy Spirit begins to work within us. When you think about it, it is very interesting. Two things occur about the same time.

1. We become convicted of our sin, and
2. We learn about the holiness of God.

Ponder that! (**Robert B. Callahan, Sr.**)

He (the Holy Spirit) convicts us, quickens us, enables us to believe, and gives us faith, produces the new nature, the rebirth in us, leads us and guides us in the process of sanctification and in many other ways. (**Martyn Lloyd-Jones**)

The Spirit will enable us to walk in righteousness, humility, faith, obedience lowliness, meekness, forbearance, love, patience, courage, praise and holiness. Our part is to count on the Spirit's presence in power to keep self on the Cross and Christ on the throne of our human personality. (**Robert B. Callahan, Sr.**)

The Lord Jesus is explicit as to what the Comforter, the Holy Spirit, will do. He will convict the world of three things: sin, righteousness, and judgment. (**Robert B. Callahan, Sr.**)

D) TRUTH

Christ's words show that nothing relating to the Holy Spirit can be learned from human reason, but that He is known only by the experience in faith. (**John Calvin**)

We vex Him [Holy Spirit] when we do not follow His guidance ... The Holy Spirit rejoices and is glad in us when we are obedient to Him in all things, and neither think nor speak anything but what is pure and holy; and on the other hand, is grieved when we give place to anything that is unworthy of our calling. (**John Calvin**)

There is one thing we must understand: God through the Holy Spirit does not work in a mechanical way. He does not force our wills. He does not compel us. However, He does persuade us, He makes the truth known to some:

A person does not believe the gospel against his will.

A person believes the gospel because he desires it, admires it, wants it, and is irresistibly drawn to it. **(Robert B. Callahan, Sr.)**

When our oldest granddaughter was three months old, I had the good fortune to spend a few minutes and unfortunately it was only 10–15 minutes with her. I carried her upstairs so I could talk to her as I packed my bag. The question came to mind; How could I or anyone grieve this child? How can anyone grieve a baby?

Then, the larger question loomed before me. How can we, who are members of the Body of Christ, grieve the Holy Spirit who was sent by the Father to dwell with us after His Son, who is our Lord and Saviour, went to the Cross, bled, suffered, and died for your sins and mine? How can we grieve Him? **(Robert B. Callahan, Sr.)**

"The ministry of the Holy Spirit, . . . is unique since it is given to all believers alike, and is permanent." **(King James Study Bible)**

Those in whom the Spirit does not reign, do not belong to Christ; therefore those who serve the flesh are not Christians, for those who separate Christ from His Spirit make Him like a dead image or corpse. We must either deny Christ, or confess that we become Christians by His Spirit. It is dreadful indeed to hear that men have so departed from the Word of the Lord, that they not only boast that they are Christians without the Spirit of God, but also ridicule the faith of others. **(John Calvin)**

How do we grieve the Holy Spirit? We grieve Him by: the works of the flesh; our words when we lie, or spew forth corrupt communications, or express anger unrighteously; our thoughts expressed in anger, jealousy, hatred, and envy; ignoring Him; failing to respond to His influence, His leadings, and His promptings; and putting ourselves first and not doing those things, which will bless ourselves and others, but more importantly glorify God. **(Robert B. Callahan, Sr.)**

This is not an ordinary truth that the Apostle Paul is describing. He is saying whatever the power of our minds may be, no matter how brilliant we may be, it is not enough. We need the Holy Spirit present and working within us before we can begin to receive and understand God's divine truth. This is hard for some to accept. We are dependent solely and exclusively upon Scripture. There is no saving truth apart from what we find in God's Holy Word. **(Robert B. Callahan, Sr.)**

The life in the Spirit is not a list of prohibitions, but a list of positive injunctions producing beneficial results. **(Robert B. Callahan, Sr.)**

E) ATTRIBUTES

Children may obey their parents in the Lord before they are able to understand any Christian doctrine; they may discharge every childish duty, under the inspiration of the Spirit of God, before they have so much as heard whether the Spirit of God has been given. **(R.W. Dale)**

A person is mistaken who hopes to obtain the Holy Spirit apart from Christ, and they are equally foolish to believe Christ can be received without the Spirit. The two go together. The One cannot be found without the other. "Paul well defines those who are endowed with the spiritual power of God as those in whom Christ dwells," as described by John Calvin. **(Robert B. Callahan, Sr.)**

How wretched we are, and devoid of all good without the power of the Holy Spirit working within us and bringing us into a right relationship with God. **(John Calvin)**

The Holy Spirit is in you. God takes up His abode in you . . . . We are not left to ourselves. **(Martyn Lloyd-Jones)**

The Holy Spirit strengthens us in the inner man, that Christ may dwell in every corner and cranny of our lives, thus emptying us of self and enthroning Christ in us as a living reality. **(Ruth Paxson)**

F) WORD

The Holy Spirit is the only true interpreter of the Word. **(William Gurnall)**

The sword is God's own utterance given to us in His written Word, inspired by the Spirit, revealed to us by the Spirit (Eph. 1:17–18), used by the Spirit in us to sanctify and cleanse, (Eph. 5:20) and then wielded by the Spirit through us to defeat the devil. (Eph. 6:17) **(Ruth Paxson)**

To let us know how necessary the graces of God's spirit are to our right using of the Word. Nothing (is) more abused than the word. And why? . . . . Because men come to it with unsound and unsanctified hearts. **(William Gurnall)**

G) WORK OF THE HOLY SPIRIT

There is only one way for a person to be a member of Christ's body, or in the common vernacular to be a Christian. They must be filled with the Spirit and have its power functioning in their daily lives. Man, meaning you and me, needs to be changed and there is only one way for that to happen, by the Holy Spirit. **(Robert B. Callahan, Sr.)**

The following describes the works of the Spirit:
- The Spirit is in the Word,
- The Spirit opens the heart,
- The Spirit is in the heart,
- The Spirit quickens us,
- The Spirit gives the faculty of belief,
- The Spirit gives a new principle to life,
- The Spirit makes all these things possible, and
- The Spirit enables us to believe.

(Robert B. Callahan, Sr.)

The Law and the prophets are not teachings handed on at the pleasure of men or produced by men's minds as their source, but are dictated by the Holy Spirit. **(John Calvin)**

The presence and the work of the Holy Spirit is necessary for an understanding of Scripture and God's revelation. **(Robert B. Callahan, Sr.)**

The flesh works, it produces work as a machine does; but the spirit produces fruit as a tree does. **(Martyn Lloyd-Jones)**

The Holy Spirit descended to form the Body of Christ. **(Ruth Paxson)**

The Spirit is not the Creator, nor is he the reconciler, but in him God shows himself to be the creator and the reconciler in that he "sanctifies" us, that is, claims us for himself and thus removes us from our power of disposal over ourselves. **(Otto Weber)**

What is the Holy Spirit telling us? That the full light of the Gospel should have a positive impact upon our faith, beliefs, attitudes, actions and practices. "A tiny spark of light led them to heaven, but now that the sun of righteousness shines on us what excuse shall we offer if we still hold to the earth or the things of the world?" **(John Calvin)**

The Holy Spirit who worked for us to implant life, now works . . . to implant power. He lives in us to strengthen and energize us with divine might . . . by a definite and continuous process. The life bestowed by the Spirit through rebirth is realized in fullness through renewal. **(Ruth Paxson)**

True evangelism is one that is utterly dependent upon the power of the Spirit to put light into man. **(Martyn Lloyd-Jones)**

Whenever the Spirit works in us, we become active in receiving, rich in our poverty, and powerful in our weakness. **(Robert B. Callahan, Sr.)**

A person cannot believe apart from the Holy Spirit. **(Robert B. Callahan, Sr.)**

During the early 1800's William Wilberforce, a devout, strong Christian, was involved in politics as well as William Pitt the Younger who for a period of time was Prime Minister.

William Pitt did not have a strong Christian faith. One Sunday, at Wilberforce's urging, William Pitt went to church. When the service was over and they were walking down the street Wilberforce exclaimed what a wonderful service it was and the impact it had on him. Pitt responded saying that he did not get anything out of it. The two men heard exactly the same message. The Holy Spirit enlightened Wilberforce, whereas He did not enlighten Pitt. (**Martyn Lloyd-Jones**)

The Holy Spirit who worked for us to implant life, now works in us to implant power. He lives in us to strengthen and energize us with divine might and by a definite and continuous process. The life bestowed by the Spirit through rebirth is realized in fullness through renewal. (**Ruth Paxson**)

He (the Holy Spirit) convicts us, quickens us, enables us to believe, produces the new nature, the rebirth in us, leads us and guides us in the process of sanctification and in many other ways. (**Martyn Lloyd-Jones**)

It is the Spirit that enlightens our hearts and minds, and provides the light to receive and enjoy the grace of God. (**Robert B. Callahan, Sr.**)

The Holy Spirit enables us to understand the Word. (**Martyn Lloyd-Jones**)

20

HUMILITY

Paul put humility first because it is the first step if we are to attain unity. Humility produces meekness which makes us patient, and by bearing with our brethren we keep that unity which would be broken a hundred times a day. (**John Calvin**)

A sense of wonder, amazement, and surprise. In other words, the true Christian does not say, 'Of course I am saved.' He says, it is an amazing thing that I should be saved at all. How did the almighty God ever bring Himself to look upon me? (**Martyn Lloyd-Jones**)

He is truly humble who neither claims anything for himself over against God, nor proudly despises his brethren, affecting superiority, but regards it sufficient to be reckoned as one of the members of Christ and desires nothing but that the Head (Christ) alone have the pre-eminence. (**John Calvin**)

How does one receive humility? Lowliness and humility are realized by: prayer; communion with God; meditating upon God's righteousness; considering our own sin; contemplating God's greatness and our limitations; God's fullness, our dependence; and God's blessings through Christ. (**Robert B. Callahan, Sr.**)

21

KINGDOM OF GOD

You cannot live the life of the Kingdom of God until you have entered the kingdom of God. You cannot share the life of the kingdom of God without being a citizen of that Kingdom. So it is wrong to talk to men who are outside the Kingdom [about] living the life of the Kingdom; it is a contradiction of the whole of the New Testament teachings. There is no greater denial of the Christian faith than just that. **(Martyn Lloyd-Jones)**

There are no different or separate ways into the Kingdom of God. There is only one way. There is only one way to have access into the presence of God and that is through the one and only Mediator. The Old Testament figures, the New Testament people, the individuals up to the present time and the ones in the future are all reconciled in and through Christ. There is no other way. This despite the teaching, by some, that many are saved in Christ, by His death and grace and at some future time the Jews will be saved by keeping the law. **(Robert B. Callahan, Sr.)**

This statement the Kingdom of God does not mean Heaven. It means entering into a relationship with God. As Calvin says, "It is rather a spiritual life, which is begun by faith in this world and daily increases according to the continual progress of faith." What is the meaning of this? No one can be truly gathered into Christ's Body and counted among the children of God until he has been renewed, or reborn. **(John Calvin)**

22

MARRIAGE

The man-woman relationship stands at the head of all other discussions. **(Markus Barth)**

Adam was taught to recognize himself in his wife, . . . and Eve, in her turn, to submit herself willingly to her husband, . . . But if the two sexes had proceeded from different sources there would have been occasion either of mutual contempt, or envy, or contentions. **(John Calvin)**

Peter wants the husbands to be prudent in discharging their responsibilities as head of the family. As Calvin points out, the husbands are to "honor their wives for nothing destroys the fellowship of life more than contempt, and we cannot really love any but those whom we esteem, so that love must be connected with respect." **(John Calvin)**

A beautiful description of the husband's love for his wife was written by Chrysostom. He says, "Hast thou seen the measure of obedience? Hear also the measure of love. Wouldst thou that thy wife shouldst obey thee as the church doth Christ? Have care thyself for her as Christ for the Church. And if it be needful that thou shouldst give thy life for her, or be cut to pieces a thousand times, or endure anything whatever, refuse it not. . . . He brought the Church to his feet by his great care, not by threats nor fear nor any such things; so do thou conduct thyself towards thy wife." **(Chrysostom)**

Each husband is to always include his wife in his thinking. He is no longer a separate unit. He does not operate or have his being apart from his other half. His wife is to be involved in all his desires. Once a man becomes a husband, he is no longer a single entity operating on his own and independently of anyone else. (**Robert B. Callahan, Sr.**)

The marriage relationship is of primary importance and takes precedence over all other human relationships. (**Robert B. Callahan, Sr.**)

The divinely appointed relationship between husband and wife with the resulting responsibility for both parties to obey God's commands. (**Ruth Paxson**)

There is an anecdote told about the Scottish evangelist John McNeil that may help us to understand this point. He traveled quite a bit and would be gone for extensive periods proclaiming the Gospel. One time when he came home tired and weary he said to his wife "who are all these children?" He had seven or eight. She responded saying, "Well, John they are your children." As mentioned he was tired and exhausted so he said to his wife, "You know, Mary, I do not know what it is, but I somehow do not realize, I do not feel that they are my children." Patiently, and lovingly she replied, "It does not matter whether you feel it or not, John, you are their father!" (**Martyn Lloyd-Jones**)

The submission of the wife to the husband in the marriage relationship is not done for the sake, or satisfaction, of her husband. That is not the reason, or the motive for so doing. It is done for Christ's sake and because it is well pleasing to Him. (**Robert B. Callahan, Sr.**)

That neither sin, nor death, nor former divisions, nor institutions, nor structures, and certainly not marriage, can escape the power and riches of grace. (**Markus Barth**)

What should be the nature and extent of the wife's subjection to the husband in their marriage? "It is not a slavish obedience to every whim and fancy of unreasonableness and selfishness on the part of the husband, but the loving and joyous subjection of loyalty to love. For the one to whom she is united as 'one flesh' she will have only respect and reverence." **(Ruth Paxson)**

God bestows the same grace alike on husbands and wives; he invites them to seek equality in them, and we know that those graces which wives share with their husbands are manifold. **(John Calvin)**

Christ submitted Himself in a self-denying, self-sacrificing love, even, unto death, for His bride, whom he cherishes and cares for in the most tender manner. The Church, the Bride, responds with the submission of absolute loyalty in yieldedness and obedience. It is the mutual submission of a pure love for a perfect lover. **(Ruth Paxson)**

The wife cannot and must not submit to the husband if it interferes with her relationship to God and the Lord Jesus Christ. **(Martyn Lloyd-Jones)**

The husbands headship entails upon him yet one more responsibility: He is to protect and provide for his wife in the same tender and loving way that Christ does for the church. **(Ruth Paxson)**

Husbands, put your ear close to this bit of God's Word; and get the full force of these words. Yours is the submission of love which partakes of both the nature and manner of Christ's love for the church, His Bride. Christ loved with a love that was utterly selfless and self-sacrificing. He loved, not thinking what He could get, but of what He could give. And, He gave all that He is and has; He gave Himself unto the uttermost, even of death. Christian husband "love your wife as." Then subjection to you on the wife's part will be only a joy and a delight. Then she will reverence you for what you truly are. **(Ruth Paxson)**

When the husband nourishes and cherishes his wife, there is much more involved than providing for the physical desire and comforts of life or satisfying tangible needs. This means that there is: nourishing and cherishing of the mind; spiritual development and growth; maturing in the Lord Jesus Christ; and enhancing and enriching the marriage itself. **(Robert B. Callahan, Sr.)**

The husbands are to "honor their wives for nothing destroys the fellowship of life more than contempt, and we cannot really love any but those we esteem, so that love must be connected with respect." (**John Calvin**)

Marriage was instituted by God. It is His ordinance. God has appointed it, ordained it, and established it for men and women, not for men and men, nor for women and women. The terms of the relationship are stated clearly and unequivocally. (**Robert B. Callahan, Sr.**)

May each husband and wife thank God, through Christ Jesus and the Holy Spirit, for enlightening Paul and revealing to him God's requirements for receiving His manifold blessings in their marriage, and may they be obedient to His commands as they continue receiving His grace upon grace. (**Robert B. Callahan, Sr.**)

This is the pattern for us to recognize, to know and to apply. It is the basis . . . for the "divinely appointed relationship between husband and wife with "the resulting responsibility for both parties to obey God's commands. (**Ruth Paxson**)

23

MERCY

We should take to heart the fact that John Calvin was beset with anxiety. William Bouwsma points out in his biography of Calvin, "He was also aware of the anxiety at the center of his life's work: he recognized in himself a terrible self-concern hardly consistent with the security he attributed to faith. 'The thought repeatedly recurs to me' he once confessed, . . . 'that I am in danger of being unjust to God's mercy by laboring with so much anxiety to assess it (God's mercy) as if it were doubtful or obscure.'" **(William Bouwsma)**

>"A Debtor to Mercy Alone"
>A debtor to mercy alone,
>Of covenant mercy I sing,
>Nor fear with the righteousness on
>My person and offering to bring,
>
>The terrors of law and of God
>With me can have nothing to do,
>My Saviour's obedience and blood
>Hide all my transgressions from view. **(Augustus Toplady)**

Paul knows the Gospel is provided through the Holy Spirit by God. He knew that men could and would stray. Therefore, he urged them to be diligent, to beware of the grievous wolves that would attack: "With a sincere heart . . . until they properly understand how much they are indebted to His mercy. And, that we should have a voluntary and cheerful love of righteousness." **(John Calvin)**

Augustine provides an excellent exposition of Paul's statement to the Corinthians, "What hast thou that thou didst not receive? now if thou didst receive it, why dost thou glory, as if thou hadst not received it?" saying that:

- It is not nature nor heredity that implants any excellence in us, nor
- Is it our own free will that enables us to procure any great talents, but
- It is God's mercy that bestows the gifts upon us.

(St. Augustine)

The Lord comes to our aid. Many foes are in arms against us, but in God's keeping we are safe. In a word, though we are brought so low that all seems over with us, yet we do not perish. You see how he turned to his own advantage every charge that the wicked (one) brings against him. **(John Calvin)**

God has chosen you to Himself, has sanctified you, and received you unto His love on the condition that you shall be merciful. **(John Calvin)**

24

OBEDIENCE

The Community of Believers can have unity with Jesus Christ only through its dependence upon Him and its obedience to Him. . . . The community is a company of people under human direction, which is fragile and sinful. It is obviously this, more than any other forms of a human community. The community is exposed to all forms and kinds of questioning. Further, the community does not have all the good or better people; it does not have all the activists or doers of good deeds, or people who accomplish great things. (**Robert B. Callahan, Sr.**)

God is properly worshipped only when we regulate all our actions according to His command, . . . since He values obedience more than sacrifice. (**John Calvin**)

(I) Count it my supreme delight to hear thy dictates and obey. (**Philip Dodderidge**)

If we claim (or profess) that we are church members (or go to church) having fellowship with God, yet walk in darkness (or according to the ways of the world), then we are liars in whom there is no truth. (**Martyn Lloyd-Jones**)

God was not saying that every obedient child would live to a ripe old age. But, He was saying that the nation's prosperity, its stability and continuance depended upon the respect and reverence the children exhibited in their attitude and actions toward their parents. Further, that the life of the family, or family life, had a direct impact upon the state. How true! **(Robert B. Callahan, Sr.)**

Obedience is the evidence of that honor which children owe to their parents and obedience is much more difficult; for the human mind recoils from subjection and only with difficulty suffers itself to be forced under the control of another. This is true of children as well as adults. **(John Calvin)**

Obey—No stronger word could be used to show that God's command to parents is to exercise parental authority, and to children to practice implicit obedience. The child that has never learned to obey parents in the home will not find it easy to obey the law of his government or the commands of his God. The obedience God requires is not merely that of action, but also of attitude, which makes a child ready to listen to his parents, willing to heed their advice and to follow the guidance of more mature minds. **(Ruth Paxson)**

People talk about going to worship God, to spending one hour a week or a month in a sanctuary and they call that worshipping God. That is not what the Apostle is talking about. "God is properly worshipped only when we regulate all our actions according to His commands, . . . since He values obedience more than sacrifice." **(John Calvin)**

For when once men have given themselves the freedom to command, they demand a strict observance of their laws and will not bear the least letter of the law to be left out either by contempt or oversight. The world is impatient of legitimate rule and especially stubborn against bearing the yoke of God. Yet it will quickly and willingly ensnare itself in empty traditions; nay, many seem to desire such slavery. And so the worship of God is vitiated, for its principle and head is obedience. The authority of men is preferred to His rule. **(John Calvin)**

We say we do not expect God to carry us to heaven on flowery beds of ease, and yet we act as if we did! The tiniest detail in which I obey has all the omnipotent power of the grace of God behind it. If I do my duty, not for duty's sake, but because I believe God is engineering my circumstances, then at the very point of my obedience the whole super grace of God is mine through the atonement. **(Robert B. Callahan, Sr.)**

What does John mean by fellowship? He does not mean an "on-again-off-again" relationship. He means we are to have a close, daily association with Christ and God. Not only that, it means knowing, accepting, and submitting to the truths of the Christian faith. As if that were not enough, this fellowship requires being obedient to God through Christ. God lays down rules and regulations for his children to follow, like a good father should, and He expects them to be obedient. May we fulfill our Father's expectations and be obedient children. **(Robert B. Callahan, Sr.)**

The children of disobedience means according to Hebrew custom the obstinate. Unbelief is always accompanied by disobedience. It is the source and mother of all stubbornness. **(John Calvin)**

Two reasons for a lack of harmony in the home are disobedience and the lack of discipline. **(Robert B. Callahan, Sr.)**

God places squarely on parents the responsibility for the instruction and training of the child in those things that make for a well-rounded full orbed Christian character and service. Such bringing up will include discipline, warnings, admonition, correction, [and] above all the teaching of God's word and fellowship in prayer around the family altar. God tells clearly how it is to be done and to what end. **(Ruth Paxson)**

25

PRAYER

Nothing less is suggested than that the life and strife of the saints be one great prayer to God, that this prayer be offered in ever new forms however, good or bad the circumstances, and that this prayer not be self-centered but express the need, and hope of all the saints. (**Markus Barth**)

Every human prayer offered with the right intention is supported by a double intercession. Think of that! Supported by the indwelling Spirit, and the glorified Christ. (**Robert B. Callahan, Sr.**)

Apollo 13 was an ill-fated space flight that had difficulty reentering the earth's orbit. There was one rocket left to make the proper reentry. This was further complicated by the fact that when the rocket was fired it required landing in the turbulent waters of the Southwest Pacific Ocean instead of touching down normally.

The weather projections were for rough seas with 22 to 23 foot waves when Apollo 13 was to splash down, which would make rescuing the crew perilous to say the least. People around the world were aware of this serious problem, the difficulties the crew would encounter. Further, they were praying for a safe landing.

Amazingly, the next day Apollo 13 splashed down into very gentle 2 to 3 foot waves making the rescue fairly simple and without fear of a mishap. The amazing power of prayer and God. (**Robert B. Callahan, Sr.**)

When everything flows on prosperously, when we are easy and cheerful, we have hardly any thought of praying; in fact, we never flee to God, unless driven by distress. Paul therefore desires us to let no season pass, without remembering to pray; so that praying at all seasons is the same as praying both in prosperity and adversity. (**John Calvin**)

The reason for exercising persistence in prayer is not that God is unwilling, but faith needs resistance before it can exercise real strength and develop according to God's will. (**Robert B. Callahan, Sr.**)

On a personal note, one Friday night while living in Pittsburgh, I developed severe stomach pains. They did not subside during the night, nor the next day. Therefore, Saturday afternoon my wife drove me to the hospital.

Fortunately, Dr. Goering was on duty. He ran several tests and had X-Rays taken. They revealed a large intestinal blockage. He explained saying, "We will have to operate." I responded, "Tomorrow I am being ordained as an elder in the First Presbyterian Church." He replied, "My wife is being ordained at the Shady Side Church tomorrow." Then, he paused and said, "We will monitor you during the night and perform additional tests tomorrow, but it appears we will have to operate."

My wife called Helen Wilson, the Fellowship Class Leader, and told her where I was and the problem. She said she would immediately have the prayer chain of approximately one hundred seventy people pray for me. Also, Ginger called Bob Lamont, the Minister, and told him about my situation. He said, "Don't worry, I'll see him tomorrow morning." And, he joined the prayer brigade.

The next morning Dr. Goering came in about 7:00 a.m. and ordered additional x-rays. About 9:00 a.m. he came to the room and said, "I don't believe it. There is no blockage. You can get dressed, go to church and be ordained."

Later that morning I began the long walk down the center aisle of the First Presbyterian Church with a queasy stomach, a faltering, hesitant step and with more than a few people having heart palpitations.

However, I made it and was ordained through the power of prayer and the caring response of a loving Father. **(Robert B. Callahan, Sr.)**

If you have not had difficulties in your prayer life then you have not begun to realize what is involved." **(Robert B. Callahan, Sr.)**

Christ asks that the Father would first sanctify the disciples; that is that He would consecrate them entirely to Himself and defend them as His sacred property. **(John Calvin)**

Prayer . . . is to fill the lungs of the soul with the oxygen of the Holy Spirit and His power. If you want to stand on your feet and not to falter fill yourself with the life of God. **(Martyn Lloyd-Jones)**

What is the relative importance of prayer in our lives?

It (prayer) is more important than knowledge and understanding. Do not imagine that I am detracting from the importance of knowledge or understanding. They are vitally important. There is only one thing . . . more important, and that is prayer. The ultimate test of my understanding of the scriptural teaching is the amount of time I spend in prayer. As theology is ultimately the knowledge of God, the more theology I know, the more it should drive me to seek to know God. Not to know about him, but to know Him. . . . If all my knowledge does not lead me to prayer there is something wrong somewhere. **(Martyn Lloyd-Jones)**

Ruth Paxson defines *"watching thereunto"* very well saying, "permitting no laziness or self-indulgence that unfits for prayer; . . . watchful for everything that feeds and fosters the prayer life, and on guard against anything that enfeebles or hinders it." **(Ruth Paxson)**

We are to watch how we pray. If our prayers are to be effective, they are to be lifted in a holy manner, expecting Him to hear and answer our prayers. **(Robert B. Callahan, Sr.)**

I remember reading about a great preacher who always wrote out his pastoral prayers for the Sunday Worship Service. When asked why, he responded by saying that he "spent time preparing his sermon for men;

therefore it was more important that he spend time preparing his prayer to God Almighty." **(Robert B. Callahan, Sr.)**

We learn from this that we rightly acknowledge the benefits of God as we ought, when we are . . . encouraged to pray that he will confirm what he has begun . . . Paul asks the faithful to pray to the Lord that his mouth may be opened (Eph. 6:19), although his voice already sounded in every place. Therefore, the more we are aware of being helped by the Lord, we should learn to ask for still greater progress . . . We must constantly pray that (The Gospel) may be continued to us. **(John Calvin)**

How are we to wrestle?
> When realizing we are going to wrestle, it is best to make preparations. Undoubtedly, each person professes to want to win the wrestling matches. Therefore, there are things to do.
>
> First, engage God by prayer to stand at thy back.
(William Gurnall)

He lays blocks before the wheel of their prayers, to try their mettle–how well they draw, when it comes a dead pull, and the mercy comes not at their prayer. **(William Gurnall)**

Prior to the War Between the States, Stonewall Jackson was a member of the First Presbyterian Church in Lexington, Virginia. One Wednesday evening he approached Dr. White, the minister, and asked if he could give the prayer next Wednesday at the mid-week service. Dr. White said he could. The next Wednesday Dr. White called on Thomas Jackson to give the prayer. He stood up, he groaned and he groaned but he could not utter any audible words and then he sat down. After the service Jackson apologized to Dr. White and asked if he could offer the prayer next Wednesday. Dr. White said he could. The results were the same. The third Wednesday Thomas Jackson offered a beautiful, meaningful prayer that everyone understood and they were uplifted by it. Dr. White said from that time forth people came on Wednesday night to hear Thomas Jackson pray. **(Robert B. Callahan, Sr.)**

Our watchfulness will do no good without prayers. **(John Calvin)**

The inarticulate groanings suggest the difficulties of shaping or forming prayers in the sinful human mind. (**Author Unknown**)

As Augustine says . . . the Apostle Paul had the thorn in the flesh, he was opposed, rejected and buffeted. He besought the Lord three times in prayer. What answer did he receive? (**St. Augustine**)

He limits His people's wishes to that principle of praying aright which subjects all our affections to the will of God. (**John Calvin**)

We are to remain connected to the Lord Jesus no matter where we are, what we are doing, or what the conditions may be. We are to stay connected through prayer. (**Georgina Dufoix**)

Should any man imitate his [Job's] patience, no doubt he will likewise feel the hand of God come at last to his relief . . . God did not allow his servant Job to be vanquished for he endured his pains with patience: So the patience of no man will be wasted . . . Why does the Apostle so greatly commend the patience of Job, who . . . showed considerable signs of impatience. The answer is, that even though on occasion he lapses through weakness of the flesh, . . . yet he always comes back to entrusting himself wholly to God, and offering himself to his restraining and controlling arm. (**John Calvin**)

He (God) limits His people's wishes to that principle of praying aright which subjects all our affections to the will of God. (**John Calvin**)

He [Christ] openly declares that He does not pray for the world, for He is solicitous only for His own flock which He received from the Father's hand . . . Christ expressly declares that they who are given to Him belong to the Father. (**John Calvin**)

When you start to take prayer seriously you begin learning something of its profound character. (**Robert B. Callahan, Sr.**)

Prayer is a duty, but it is much more than a duty. It should be a delight, it should be the ultimate expression of the Christian life. (**Martyn Lloyd-Jones**)

While members of the First Presbyterian Church in Pittsburgh we were truly blessed due to the prayer life of the Fellowship Class. Some wonderful and amazing things happened during that ten year period.

Our teacher was a lady named Helen Wilson. She was a retired schoolteacher and must have been an excellent one according to her former students. Her major was English. On one occasion she told us about her Father who had been an uneducated person, especially by today's standards. She related how he used horrible grammar when he spoke, yet he was a man of prayer. He believed in prayer. He practiced prayer. Helen told us she never once heard him make a grammatical error when he was praying. The power of the Holy Spirit. **(Robert B. Callahan, Sr.)**

There is another interesting point in the Master's prayer. He does not ask that we be taken out of the world, or that a fence be erected around us, or that we have a special position. He does not pray that we have a life of ease or pleasure, or that all our troubles, afflictions, problems, harassments, go away and never reappear. Nor, does he pray to remove all anxieties or negative circumstances from our lives. Though those things may beset us, our focus is to be upon the object of our faith, none other than the Lord Jesus Christ. Our eyeballs are not to be turned inwardly, but to seek, search and find the Lord of the universe. His strength will sustain us. **(Robert B. Callahan, Sr.)**

We cannot truly pray without the Holy Spirit, and true prayer is always by the Holy Spirit through the Lord Jesus Christ. **(Robert B. Callahan, Sr.)**

The boldness which the apostles had was as "The child of prayer, it was not bred in them, but it was granted from heaven to them" **(William Gurnall)**

The Apostle (Paul) prays that God grant us according to the riches of His glory that we will be strengthened with might by His Spirit. He prays that the Holy Spirit will work in our hearts, minds, and wills. We need to be strengthened so we can comprehend the great truths of Christ, so that we can grasp hold of them, and not allow them to elude us. **(Robert B. Callahan, Sr.)**

There is an obligation imposed upon us as members of Christ's body to pray and watch. A Christian [is] to watch . . . that he may keep the Lord's charge and do the duty imposed upon him as a Christian . . . . This is not a temporary duty, but for his whole lifetime. **(William Gurnall)**

Paul's prayer (Eph. 3:14–19) is a marvelous example of how we should pray: bowing to the Father; praying for others; having Christ dwell in our hearts; being rooted and grounded in love; comprehending with all the saints; knowing the love of Christ; and being filled with all the fullness of God. **(Robert B. Callahan, Sr.)**

We are to pray to God expectantly. However, we may have to learn to pray. This requires time, effort, and understanding. Yes, we are to ask and to expect, but we are to be guided by God's will, as given in the Word written and the Word incarnate. That puts a different connotation on praying expectantly. **(Robert B. Callahan, Sr.)**

26

PREACHING / TEACHING

Before proceeding I would like to note the life in Christ is not one of morality or ethics or standards. The preaching and teaching of these items as being Christian is a contradiction of the New Testament. Matthew Arnold sums it up very accurately and succinctly, "It has been the preaching of the good life, of being a good little gentleman, and of viewing religion as morality touched by emotion that has been the curse." (**Matthew Arnold**)

Paul denies that he ever refrained from telling people those things that were for their benefit. Therefore, we should appreciate the fact that a pure, candid, and straightforward presentation of sound doctrine is required from Christ's servants. (**Robert B. Callahan, Sr.**)

Some ministers gloss over the blood of the new covenant in our communion services. The seminaries stress other points, and people like to hear about what they can do, not what Christ has done. (**Robert B. Callahan, Sr.**)

God's plan is to redeem everyone and to reunite everything through Christ. God has purposed to restore all things in Christ. (**Robert B. Callahan, Sr.**)

A dignitary of the Roman Catholic Church was asked, in private, why their policy on Scripture had been changed. His reply is worth noting. He said, "I will tell you why we have changed our policy. There is no longer any need for us to be afraid of the scriptures, for this reason, that you Protestants no longer believe in the scriptures. It is you Protestants with your destructive criticism of the scriptures that have undermined the confidence of the people in the scriptures. So we are able to say that it is we alone who are standing for the scriptures." **(Martyn Lloyd-Jones)**

It is the fundamental business of preaching and teaching that the hearers eyes should be opened, not that they should be entertained. They are to go from darkness to light and knowledge. **(Robert B. Callahan, Sr.)**

Preachers and teachers are not to continually feed their members with milk and honey. They are to serve meat, some tough meat, as well as some tart food, and even some vinegar. The teacher is to serve a balanced diet and the students are to ingest it. **(Robert B. Callahan, Sr.)**

These precepts, which imply not only the possibility, but the existence of such gross immoralities in the character and the conduct of those to whom they were addressed, were meant for the very same persons that Paul had described as "saints" and "the faithful in Christ Jesus." **(R.W. Dale)**

The fare that I shall be serving during the coming weeks will be from God's own table. If perchance it does not go down well or should not have the flavor that you desire, please do not despise the provider of the food but blame the cook who has prepared it and is serving it. **(William Gurnall)**

Ministers of the church are ambassadors for testifying and proclaiming the blessing of reconciliation only on the condition that they speak from the gospel as providing a legitimate warrant for what they say. **(John Calvin)**

Prophets and teachers have a most formidable task. They are to acquire skill, experience and knowledge in order as Calvin says, "to make known the will of God, by applying prophecies, threats, promises, and all the teachings of Scripture to the current needs of the called out." **(John Calvin)**

Our stomachs and bodies are fed by the food we ingest. Some is good for us, some is not. Our hearts, minds and souls are fed by the teachings we ingest. Some good, some not. Therefore, we have to be selective and accept that which is good for us. "Our souls are fed by the teaching of the Gospel, when it is efficacious by the power of the Spirit. Therefore, as faith is the life of the soul, all that nourishes and advances faith is compared to food." **(John Calvin)**

It is not the primary objective of preaching and teaching to just exhort and comfort people. It should be a basic objective to instruct the hearers, because it is only as one grasps the doctrines of faith, in Christ, that a person can truly live and enjoy life as one is meant to do. **(Robert B. Callahan, Sr.)**

That his (Paul's) teaching of Christ was not changeable or ambiguous, so as to present Christ in different shapes at different times . . . others, to please men, present Christ under different false disguises, and others again teach a thing one day and the next retract it, out of fear. Such was not Paul's Christ nor the Christ of any apostle . . . For the only true Christ is He in whom can be seen this invariable and perpetual 'yea' which Paul here declares to be characteristic of Him. **(John Calvin)**

All real and effective teaching must be in harmony with truth as truth is in Him. **(R.W. Dale)**

The vainglorious person, the one who wants to make known his or her ideas, who is witty or wishes to orate instead of making known the Gospel and opening the Scriptures so they can be applied. **(William Gurnall)**

God never laid it upon thee to convert those he sends to thee, No; to publish the gospel is thy duty, to receive it is theirs. **(William Gurnall)**

"My people are destroyed for lack of knowledge: because thou hast rejected knowledge, I will also reject thee, that thou shalt be no priest to me: seeing thou hast forgotten the law of thy God, I will also forget thy children." **[Hos. 4:6]**

These are examples of what we must do. We must exert the effort, but the strength, power and might come from the Lord. This is different from what some modern teachings would lead us to believe. "The Bible is full of exhortations, and appeals and arguments and demonstrations and reasonings. . . . These New Testament teachings would never have been necessary at all if that other teaching were correct. All the Apostles would have had to say . . . Now then, you have been converted, you have been saved, you have been justified. That is step number one." **(Martyn Lloyd-Jones)**

Scripture must be the norm for all teaching. It is the only basis for proper teaching and instruction. This means the whole of Scripture, not just selected portions. We need to learn the negatives, as well as the positives, the plusses and the minuses, and what we are to do as well as what we are not to do. **(Robert B. Callahan, Sr.)**

Christ is the foundation upon which the teaching and learning are to take place. This is important, the teaching and learning are to take place only upon the one true foundation, that being Jesus Christ Himself. **(Robert B. Callahan, Sr.)**

Christ, by exercising His power toward you in my teaching, has proved that He speaks through my mouth so that there is no excuse for your ignorance. **(John Calvin)**

Unfortunately, too often in today's world the control of the church at various levels is in the hands of those who are wise in the ways of the world and strangers to the purposes of God as revealed in Christ Jesus. The ways of the world are adopted and espoused, while the ways of the Lord are ignored or relegated to a secondary position. **(Robert B. Callahan, Sr.)**

Preachers and teachers need to remember what Paul knew so well that God judged him according to the content of the message he proclaimed and his faithfulness in delivering it. He judges us by our: faithfulness in hearing the Word and applying it; obedience to His commands and teachings; and perseverence in praying for all the saints. **(Robert B. Callahan, Sr.)**

Paul preaches and teaches the gospel as the power of God, as spiritual dynamite that can operate in men and change them. **(Martyn Lloyd-Jones)**

True evangelism is one that is utterly dependent upon the power of the Spirit to put light into man. We need to be made light and we need to be enlightened. **(Martyn Lloyd-Jones)**

What do we really need? It is this knowledge of God, of the attributes of God, His glory, His ineffability, His holiness, His almightiness, His eternity, His omniscience, His omnipresence, that is what we really need. **(Martyn Lloyd-Jones)**

The mere fact that there are difficulties in the Scripture does not mean that we should bypass them. **(Martyn Lloyd-Jones)**

The Christian teaching realizes that it cannot transform society as a whole; it must go on trusting that gradually the teaching will act as a leaven, and that men will become more and more enlightened. The time lag is not to be explained in terms of the failure of biblical teachings; it is to be explained in terms of the blindness of the world to Christian teaching. Christians have been given wisdom by God and the power to be patient and to wait until the right time for action has arrived. **(Martyn Lloyd-Jones)**

The evil started with the priests, but the people, due to their own sins, deserved to have corrupt and degraded pastors. Therefore, they all contributed to infecting one another and to turning against God. Woe unto those who do not teach and preach God's word, who focus on works, but not on the gospel of Christ, and His shed blood. It is as true today as it was then. Nothing has really changed. **(Robert B. Callahan, Sr.)**

What really matters is the spiritual truths as given by the Holy Spirit. Think of Jeremiah, the majority in his time had gone wrong. They had left the teachings of God. But, Jeremiah knew the truth and spoke the truth as it was revealed to him. He did not say the popular things. He did not like his role, nor being unpopular, nor being disliked, nor being laughed at, nor being ridiculed, but he proclaimed the Word of God.

And in proclaiming it he had to endure the abuses and taunts of men. **(Robert B. Callahan, Sr.)**

I do not find the Apostle telling me to hand it over to the Lord and that He will fight my battles for me while I just sit back and enjoy the fruit of His victory. It is not here! I have to fight! **(Martyn Lloyd-Jones)**

There will be no fight, there will be no struggle, effort will not be required. So when they find that, on the contrary, they have grave difficulties and a mighty battle they are utterly discouraged. **(Martyn Lloyd-Jones)**

The next thing it is not, is that a person's life is more important than what he or she believes. People may say that a certain person is not a Christian, but their good deeds prove they are. Balderdash! What a person believes does make a difference. To tell people that what a man believes does not matter as long as he lives a good life and does good is not only a denial of the gospel, it is bound to discourage people from believing the only truth which can save them. **(Martyn Lloyd-Jones)**

The ultimate way to test whether a man is truly preaching the gospel or not, is to notice the emphasis which he places on the blood. **(Charles Spurgeon)**

If religious truth does not meet the just demands of the intellect as well as of the moral nature, it will be regarded with languid interest and will at last be either silently abandoned or rejected with open hostility and scorn. **(R.W. Dale)**

A mission station and hospital in China had problems, unrest, and disobedience.

> Then there was a revival as a result of preaching and teaching the word and the Holy Spirit working among the people.
> The missionary wrote our hospital is no more like it used to be. There is perfect harmony among all the hospital workers from servants up. All do faithful work. I never have to reprove any of them. I even never have to tell servants what to do. All know their work and do it faithfully. **(Ruth Paxson)**

The preaching and teaching of the Word among men is to be complete and full. The preaching and teaching of the Word serves the needs of the people. The community of believers is a mirror in which the angels contemplate the magnificent wisdom of God which they had not known previously. The angels saw new works which had been hidden in God, and it is in this way that they progress. (**Robert B. Callahan, Sr.**)

Teaching is the duty of all pastors; but there is a particular gift of interpreting scripture, so that sound doctrine may be kept and a man may be doctor (teacher) who is not fitted to preach. (**John Calvin**)

There is nothing so insidious in the realm of Christendom, nothing so injurious to the body of Christ, nothing further from the teachings of Scripture than that adults do not have to study Christ's teachings and apply themselves to His teachings. No, that is not the teaching of our Master. (**Robert B. Callahan, Sr.**)

The righteousness of God is revealed from faith to faith, from the faith of one believer to the faith of another, but the wrath of God is revealed from heaven. The Holy Spirit has bestowed upon preachers and teachers the ability to tell people of God's grace, to proclaim the Gospel, and to communicate the faith, but the wrath is from heaven, therefore, it is to be proclaimed by preachers and teachers.

When considering God's Word, bear in mind, it is a "privilege" to announce faith and righteousness, but it is a duty to announce wrath and unrighteousness. (**Robert B. Callahan, Sr.**)

The places on which they treat were plain till they expounded them. Their text was clear till their obscure discourse darkened it. (**Unknown**)

Paul is ever-bold in proclaiming the Gospel and ever-loving in caring for the saints. (**Robert B. Callahan, Sr.**)

Ministers of the church are ambassadors for testifying and proclaiming the blessing of reconciliation only on the condition that they speak from the Gospel as providing a legitimate warrant for what they say. (**John Calvin**)

Paul presented the gospel in the following ways:
- He fed them with the full doctrine;
- He fed them with the details of how they were to walk;
- He fed them the miracles, teachings, and truths of Christ and Him crucified;
- He did not hesitate, he did not apologize, he proceeded on course;
- He wanted to proclaim the gospel, all aspects of it;
- He wanted them to hear it, because he knew if they heard it, that it would change their lives;
- He wanted them to be able to handle the triumphs and defeats of life; and
- He wanted to serve God, not to please men.

(Robert B. Callahan, Sr.)

The teacher, whether he be the pastor or another has the responsibility to provide instruction in the doctrine and truth as it is found and revealed in the Lord Jesus Christ. **(Robert B. Callahan, Sr.)**

The urgency, knowledge and love of God's will, will not be felt immediately in every area of one's life. Moral distinctions which were once non-existent or at best very faint will not become vivid overnight. **(Robert B. Callahan, Sr.)**

There is no teaching so harmful or adverse to our souls, to a right relationship with God, than the universal Fatherhood of God, and that Jesus did not need to come into the world to shed His blood, die on the Cross, and atone for our sins and sinfulness. **(Robert B. Callahan, Sr.)**

The message is to be the precise truth about God, the Lord Jesus Christ, the Holy Ghost and the way of salvation. **(Robert B. Callahan, Sr.)**

Christ selected people to teach the Gospel who would be faithful witnesses. Those selected were motivated to have fellowship with one another in His name and to receive the blessings available from God through His Son. These factors had a significant impact not only in hearing the Word, but in communicating it. They contributed immeasurably to increasing one's faith and witness, and to applying the Master's teachings. **(Robert B. Callahan, Sr.)**

Therefore, we are to state the truth clearly and precisely in order to help others. We do not want to show that we are right and they are wrong, but to present the truth and have the Holy Spirit interpret it aright in their hearts. We are to speak with humility. We are to explain and to expound. We are to have compassion and sympathy. We are to exercise great patience. We are not to do anything that will offend another or that will prove a hindrance to another. We are to express the truth and allow the Holy Spirit to reveal it to the hearers so that they will grasp it and accept it. We are to try to enlighten them. Error is to be exposed! **(Robert B. Callahan, Sr.)**

The most important factor in the life or existence of the community of believers, more important than any so-called accomplishments or achievements that may be identified or described or boasted about, is that the community in its speaking, acting, and serving must point beyond itself. It must ever and always point to the centrality of Christ. It must continually point to Christ as its Lord, Head, and Shepherd, to the obedient servant with the crown of thorns going to Calvary's Hill and shedding His blood. All other activities, proclamations, and urgings pale in comparison to what Christ did. We are "in Christ" and we are members of the community. Therefore, our obedience is to be to God's will and in accord with Christ's teachings. **(Robert B. Callahan, Sr.)**

What God declares in Ezekiel about His prophet, applies to pastors and teachers today. It explicitly says we are responsible if any perish due to our negligence or ignorance in presenting the Gospel. The account is to be paid by us, and those who go astray will be charged to us. That is an awesome responsibility to those who preach and teach! **(Robert B. Callahan, Sr.)**

He [God] presents facts, truths and reasons. We ignore them to our own detriment. Probably, there is nothing so insidious in the realm of Christendom, nothing so injurious to the body of Christ, nothing further from the teachings of Scripture than that adults do not have to study

Christ's teachings, do not have to apply themselves, and that all they have to do once a week, or once a month, or when convenient, is to go to church, contribute a little time or money, or go to a church supper. NO, that is not the teaching of our Master. Unfortunately, ministers or teachers who do not proclaim the whole Gospel do much harm to furthering the witness of the Lord Jesus Christ and to presenting the truth to both the believer and the non-believer. **(Robert B. Callahan, Sr.)**

Preachers and teachers for the most part wish to present the pleasant accounts and teachings of Scripture, and to overstress the love of God, but that is not according to God's divine revelation presented in His Word. We, the teachers and pastors, have no right to interpose our choices and priorities over divine revelation. **(Robert B. Callahan, Sr.)**

Peter warns us about false teachers saying, *"Who privily shall bring in damnable heresies."* That is strong language. The word *privily* means to bring in secretly or unaware, as bringing in spies or traitors. They come clothed as sheep, but they are ravenous wolves. Knowingly or unknowingly, they distort or pervert the truths of Christ. Those *damnable heresies* mean leading one to division and ruin. They do so by:

- Being part of a respected church, organization, or institution;
- Stating that this is what a certain seminary, or group has to say, and,
- Denying the words of our Master indirectly, or by innuendo, or by saying people are different in this day and time.

The true members of Christ's body are to be knowledgeable about the teachings in Scripture, and to be on guard against Satan's subtle innuendos. **(Robert B. Callahan, Sr.)**

To tell people that what a man believes does not matter as long as he lives a good life and does good is not only a denial of the gospel, it is bound to discourage people from believing the only truth which can save them. **(Martyn Lloyd-Jones)**

27

REDEMPTION / SALVATION

The Apostle John uses the word 'cleanseth' or 'cleanse.' It is a verb and it is used in the present tense to signify that the cleansing action is a continuous one. It means that the blood of Christ keeps on cleansing us! Though we do not do as we would, and do as we would not, the cleansing keeps occurring. It does not stop. **(Martyn Lloyd-Jones)**

In Christology the issue is not a change of our consciousness, but the transformation of the realm of lordship and thus of the very structure of life. Jesus Christ is not the object of our knowledge but the giver of new life. Therefore Christology is never just the "knowledge of God the redeemer" but simultaneously the experience of a turning around in our existence. **(Otto Weber)**

Redemption–is ultimately going to end in the glorification of my body; but it begins with forgiveness and continues to emphasize it. **(Martyn Lloyd-Jones)**

When you receive the gift of salvation you become alive unto God, to the things of God, the commands of God, fellowship with God and communicating with God. **(Robert B. Callahan, Sr.)**

What does Paul mean? He is not talking of our physical birth. But, he is asserting that we are new creatures and have been formed, made, unto righteousness.

How? By the spirit of Christ Jesus, not by our own strength or power. This applies to the believers, who have been spiritually regenerated by God's grace and who begin to become new people. Therefore, everything that is good in us is the work of God. We are God's work because we have been created in Christ; we are no longer in Adam.

This is a most wonderful, yet profound statement. We cannot just gloss over it. Think for a moment of the many, many things you do in a day, week or year and how many times you gloss over items or take the hit or miss approach. Yet, here is God in all His majesty and splendor and what does He do? He works within us, He makes us His workmanship. He performs a creative act within us through Christ Jesus unto good works. WE ARE HIS WORKMANSHIP. (**Robert B. Callahan, Sr.**)

The highest manifestation of the glory of God is His love as we receive it through His redemption. (**Robert B. Callahan, Sr.**)

Actually the phrase "who hold the truth in unrighteousness" means "to hold the truth of God unjustly and unworthily." (**Robert B. Callahan, Sr.**)

Paul believing in the "unsearchable riches of Christ," knew that:
- For human sin there is divine forgiveness;
- For human weakness there is divine redemption;
- For human uncertainty and doubt there is divine illumination;
- For human fears and needs there is free access to God; and
- For human limitations and restless discontent there is ineffable strength, righteousness and mercy in our union with the Lord Jesus Christ.

   (**Robert B. Callahan, Sr.**)

If you ... look at the 20th and 21st verses in this 4th chapter of Ephesians you will note in the 20th verse that Paul says Christ and then in the 21st verse he says Jesus. Why the difference? Paul is trying to teach us a very important truth. He does not want us to talk or think about some great cosmic Christ who exerts undue influence upon people in this world, nor does he want us to think of salvation in loose or vague terms, or to think of salvation as some idea or concept that is neither practical nor applicable. The Apostle wants us to think in the terms of something real, something touchable and something near. Therefore he says, *"as the truth is in Jesus."* Paul knows that we are saved by the person Jesus. Not by any other way, idea or philosophy. (**Robert B. Callahan, Sr.**)

"If we wish to be Christ's, we must be regenerated by God, but this is no ordinary gift. In this context the Apostle is speaking of the grace of regeneration that God confers upon His elect as the Creator of the Church and in so doing He refashions them into His own image." *This truth should humble us and make us realize what we are to give to God who has made us into new creatures.* (**John Calvin**)

Ministers of the church are ambassadors for testifying and proclaiming the blessing of reconciliation only on the condition that they speak from the Gospel as providing a legiti- mate warrant for what they say. (**John Calvin**)

Paul sheds additional light on salvation through Christ when he says, *"And you, being dead in your sins and the uncircumcision of your flesh, hath he quickened (made alive) together with him, having forgiven you all trespasses; Blotting out the handwriting (certificate of debt) of ordinances that was against us, which was contrary to us, and took it out of the way, nailing it to his cross; And having spoiled (disarmed) principalities and powers, he made a show (spectacle) of them openly, triumphing over them in it."* [**Col. 2:13–15**]

However severe and wrathful a judge God shows Himself to be towards unbelievers (and believers) whenever He punishes them, His primary purpose is to provide counsel for their salvation and to have them come into a right relationship with Himself. This is one way by which He demonstrates His fatherly love. (**John Calvin**)

There is a very significant fact about our life in Christ or the Christian faith. What we commonly call Christianity at the beginning of the 21st Century is composed of several things, which are:

- It is the pronouncement of certain facts and events that have taken place;

- Second, it tells us that our salvation, or right relationship to God is based upon them;
- Third, in the fullness of time God sent forth His only begotten Son, made of a woman, made under the law, to redeem us;
- Fourth, that Son was Jesus of Nazareth and He is essential; and,
- Fifth, we are not saved by applying His teachings, but by Him.

Therefore, we are intimately, inextricably tied to the truth as it is in Jesus.

The Apostle Paul uses the name Jesus by itself very seldom in his letters. However, he does in this instance. **(Robert B. Callahan, Sr.)**

Man' reconciliation by God's grace is inseparable from God's confidence and command that man be reconciled. Think of that: God's confidence and command that we be reconciled. **(Markus Barth)**

Hope is a supernatural grace of God, whereby the believer, through Christ expects and waits for all those good things of the promise, which at present he hath not received, or not fully. **(William Gurnall)**

We have been transferred from the deepest hell to heaven itself. **(John Calvin)**

One fact to realize is that salvation is God's plan, not ours. If we are participating in it then we should follow the commands of the Captain. He is the one who decides what is to be done. We not only receive our orders from Him, but He prepares and guides us. Also, He provides the necessary strength. **(Martyn Lloyd-Jones)**

We have no right to pick and choose. God's way of salvation takes up the intellect, the heart (emotions), the will, the understanding, the sensibilities, the experience, the practice, everything, the whole man. **(Martyn Lloyd-Jones)**

We are to learn and to understand that the first objective in salvation has to do with the glory of God. Please do not misunderstand or completely misinterpret what I am saying, but the primary intent with salvation is not us–it is God and His glory. That is the teaching of Scripture.

We are not to start with our own sins or acts, but with our condition in sin. We are to learn and know about the condition of men in sin. The condition that has been true through the ages. We are to realize what has been true of man apart from Christ. **(Robert B. Callahan, Sr.)**

It means that the blood of Christ keeps on cleansing us! Though we do not do as we would, and do as we would not, the cleansing keeps occurring. It does not stop. **(Martyn Lloyd-Jones)**

Many people think the day of giving an account will never come . . . These people should remember the day of the Crucifixion: when Christ was scourged, as he climbed Calvary's Hill; when He shed His blood and died. Yes, we are to remember that day. But thank God the third day came when He rose from the dead. The day of giving an account will come. **(Robert B. Callahan, Sr.)**

Men should be carefully warned that righteousness and salvation are obtained by Christ's death that we may become God's holy possession. **(John Calvin)**

Christ is salvation and our salvation is in Him. **(Robert B. Callahan, Sr.)**

We need to realize and accept the fact a person (a believer) never stands before God by himself or herself. The individual is never dependent upon his own actions. He or she is dependent upon Christ and thank God for that. **(Robert B. Callahan, Sr.)**

Man's reconciliation by God's grace is inseparable from God's confidence and command that man 'be reconciled.' Think of that–God's confidence and command. **(Markus Barth)**

As we conclude our consideration of boldness, access and confidence it is beneficial to examine Calvin's teaching about Christ, our salvation, doctrine and its application. He says:

- "We see that our whole salvation and all its parts are comprehended in Christ (**Acts 4:12**),
- We should not derive the least potion from anywhere else,
- If we seek salvation, we are taught by the very name of Jesus, that it is 'of him.' (**1 Cor 1:30**)
- If we seek strength, it is in His dominion,
- If purity, in his conception,
- If gentleness, in His birth, (**Heb 2:17**)
- If we seek redemption, it is in His passion,
- If acquittal, in His condemnation,
- If remission of the curse, in His Cross (**Gal 3:13**)
- If satisfaction, in His sacrifice,
- If purification, in His blood,
- If reconciliation, in His descent into hell,
- If mortification of the flesh, in His tomb,
- If newness of life, in His resurrection,
- If immortality, in the same,
- If inheritance of the Heavenly Kingdom, in His entrance into Heaven,
- If protection, security, and an abundant supply of blessings, in His Kingdom,
- If untroubled expectation of judgment, in the power given to Him to judge."

(John Calvin)

Knowledge of full salvation in Christ is absolutely essential for the Christian warrior. If he has any doubt of his own salvation: how can he effectually win a sinner to Christ? And in these days of manifold Satanic counterfeits, how can he discern the false from the true? **(Ruth Paxson)**

It is hard, it is slow to reach the point in life where we can accept, "The troubles of this life are so far from hindering our salvation that they rather assist it." **(John Calvin)**

There is much less ground for tolerating the ignorance of people who think the Gospel is offered universally to all men in such a way that it is free to everyone without distinction to lay hold of salvation by faith. **(John Calvin)**

What is the primary intent and objective of salvation?

> It is not what most people think. It is not me, it is not you. But, it is the glory of God. God does this in order to provide a witness and demonstration to His glory. He does it to manifest His own glory. **(Robert B. Callahan, Sr.)**

The blessed Trinity is concerned about our salvation and the three persons who have worked and are working for our salvation. They are working to bring us into a right relationship with the Father in order that we might have fellowship with Him. That is the purpose of our salvation, not just our eternal existence. May I repeat that? The purpose of our salvation is not just our eternal existence, but having a right relationship with God the Father. **(Robert B. Callahan, Sr.)**

The end of salvation is that we glorify Christ by becoming holy because of what He has done, not because of any works, contributions, or merit on our part. **(Robert B. Callahan, Sr.)**

The mind is integral and paramount to being in a right relationship to God in Christ, . . . and knowing the hope of salvation. The Apostle (Paul) is concerned with the attitude of the saints and faithful regarding their faith in Christ and the negatives encountered in walking *worthy of the vocation* (calling) *wherewith ye are called.* He realized the saints and faithful would be tormented by disappointments, disheartenments, weariness, tiredness, opposition, and hopelessness. Therefore, the Apostle says, . . .And let us not be weary in well doing; for in due season we shall reap, if we faint not (do not lose heart). **(Robert B. Callahan, Sr.)**

Yes, there are rewards for good works, but, this teaching does not replace or supersede the teaching that salvation . . . is by grace and the free gift of God. "Evil deeds are given the punishment they deserve, but in rewarding good deeds, [He] does not have regard to their merit or worth. No work of ours is so full and complete in all its parts as to deserve God's approval." **(John Calvin)**

People talk about going to worship God, to spending one hour a week or a month in a sanctuary and they call that worshipping God. That is not what the Apostle is talking about. "God is properly worshipped only when we regulate all our actions according to His command, . . . since He values obedience more than sacrifice." **(John Calvin)**

When considering these truths, bear in mind, that what he means by this is, reconciliation is not taken from something that resides within a person or has been laying dormant since natural birth. Rather, it is something that comes from the outside, something that enters into a person, and makes him a new creature. **(Robert B. Callahan, Sr.)**

Without the shedding of blood there is no remission of sins. **(Robert B. Callahan, Sr.)**

Salvation is to **Walk with God,** in gratitude and humility, to walk in the light, not in darkness. **(Robert B. Callahan, Sr.)**

If God had not allowed the possibility of man's fall then there would have been limitations on man's freedom. If there had been limitations, man would not have been created perfectly by God. Man as created by God had free will, but he lost it by falling into sin. However, no matter what the explanation, it is perfectly clear that God has overruled it through His redemption and in so doing has displayed certain attributes of His Holy being, nature, and character. Otherwise these things would never have been known. **(Robert B. Callahan, Sr.)**

It is not that our sins are condoned or forgotten because we have been baptized and united with Christ; our sins are erased **only** because of what Christ did for us on the Cross by shedding **His** blood. **(Robert B. Callahan, Sr.)**

Before I could draw nigh to God something had to be done about my sins and my sinful condition. That something was the shed blood of Christ. **(Robert B. Callahan, Sr.)**

The blessed Trinity is concerned about our salvation. They work to bring us into a right relationship with the Father in order that we might have fellowship with Him. That is the purpose of our salvation, *not just our eternal existence.* (**Robert B. Callahan, Sr.**)

28

REVELATION

During the early 1800's William Wilberforce, a devout, strong Christian, was involved in politics as well as William Pitt the Younger who for a period of time was Prime Minister.

> William Pitt did not have a strong Christian faith. One Sunday, at Wilberforce's urging, William Pitt went to church. When the service was over and they were walking down the street Wilberforce exclaimed what a wonderful service it was and the impact it had on him. Pitt responded saying that he did not get anything out of it. The two men heard exactly the same message. The Holy Spirit enlightened Wilberforce, whereas He did not enlighten Pitt. (**Martyn Lloyd-Jones**)

Lord Jesus, make thyself to me,
A living bright reality;
More present to faith's vision,
More keen than any outward object seen;
More dear, more intimately nigh
Than e'en the sweetest earthly tie. (**Hudson Taylor**)

What God has given to be known is known. (**Otto Weber**)

We are only able to understand the knowledge of God, . . . because God himself discloses and has disclosed Himself as a person: In Jesus Christ through the Holy Spirit. Further, Weber says–in terms of substance and being "revelation unconditionally precedes knowledge." (**Otto Weber**)

Patiently God, through our history, accommodates his ways of revelation to our condition. Thus, par excellence, the Word made flesh and the written Word from which he speaks is God accommodating himself to us. **(Ford Lewis Battles)**

The prophets to whom he (Paul) is referring are those who are: Blessed with the unique gift of dealing with Scripture, not only by interpreting it, but also by the wisdom they show in making it meet the needs of the hour. **(John Calvin)**

29

RIGHTEOUSNESS

The Lord Jesus Christ teaches us about God. Yes, he makes us conscious of our sinfulness, but He also makes us aware of the righteousness that is available in Him. When you believe on the Lord Jesus Christ your sins are forgiven and you are clothed with the righteousness of Christ. Therefore, you can go into the presence of God, because of Christ's righteousness, not yours. He atoned for your sins by His death. His obedience is imputed to us for righteousness. This righteousness is part of the unsearchable riches of Christ. (**Robert B. Callahan, Sr.**)

We are to seek for righteousness only from God; . . . and the sum of all our blessings is laid up for us and daily offered to us, in none but Christ . . . The soul is regenerated, . . . by that saving knowledge of God and of Christ. (**John Calvin**)

The righteousness of God does not mean the righteousness that God gives us, but rather it means the righteousness of God that makes us acceptable to Him. (**Robert B. Callahan, Sr.**)

Righteousness comes from and through the Messiah. No one except the Messiah can and will establish it among his people . . . it is a gift of God! (**Markus Barth**)

These verses reveal that the godly "truly and sincerely fear God and desire to submit to His righteousness. However, the ungodly, those who have an evil conscience, those who do not fear God, and worship Him, they are not heard when they do call upon God." **(John Calvin)**

Had man kept his primitive righteousness, Christ's pain and pains would have been spared. It was because of man's lost holiness that he came to recover . . . both God and man, between whom Christ comes to negotiate, call for holiness. God's glory and man's happiness; neither of which can be attained except holiness be restored to man. **(William Gurnall)**

Normally, Christian righteousness is achieved slowly. The fruit of the Spirit has to ripen according to God's plan and way. There is the growth, the bud, the flower, the fruit beginning to appear, the rain, the sun, the cold, the heat, the days and nights, then the maturing of the fruit and at last the availability, sharing, and enjoying of it. And, one other thing, the planting of the seed so that more fruit will be borne. **(Robert B. Callahan, Sr.)**

Righteousness produces the fruit of holiness and eternal life. The gift of God is our justification and the fruit of the Spirit is our sanctification. **(Robert B. Callahan, Sr.)**

The righteousness of grace is received in two ways:
1. "Imputed righteousness, which is wrought by Christ for the believer," and
2. "Imparted righteousness, which is wrought by Christ in the believer."

    This righteousness of grace is wrought for the believer and in the believer. Gurnall amplifies upon this by stating that, "The imputed righteousness, is the righteousness of our justification, by which the believer stands just and righteous before God and is called, . . . the righteousness of God."

    This imparted righteousness is, as Gurnall says, "not only wrought by Christ, but also performed in Christ, who is God, and is not inherent in us, though for us, so that the benefit of it rebounds by faith to us, as if we had wrought it." **(William Gurnall)**

We are to seek for righteousness only from God; . . . and the sum of all our blessings is laid up for us and daily offered to us, in none but Christ

... The soul is regenerated, ... by that saving knowledge of God and of Christ. **(John Calvin)**

In these two verses (1 John 2:1, 2) John clearly states what Christ does for us. The flesh is weak. Therefore, it is important to know as Calvin said that "men should be carefully warned that righteousness and salvation are obtained by Christ's death that we may become God's holy possession!" That is why we have an advocate with the Father. We are far from being righteous, but His righteousness is imputed and imparted to us. This is done for all who truly believe in Him and are members of His body.

> Then, John tells us to *"abide in him"* and to *"know that he is righteous"* and to *"know that every one that doeth righteousness is born of Him:"* [1 John 2:28, 29]
>
> The Apostle wants to make us aware of the living presence of Christ and as Calvin says to have "a real sense of His power which begets confidence."
>
> It is one thing to feel something, but it is entirely different to know it and to have complete confidence in it. That is why, Calvin also says, "the godly calmly wait for Christ and do not dread His presence." **(Robert B. Callahan, Sr.)**

Righteousness is to exhibit itself in righteous action. Those who believe on the Lord Jesus Christ are brought into a right relationship with God. **(Robert B. Callahan, Sr.)**

There is an "imparted righteousness." This begins where the imputed righteousness leaves off. God "now begins to work in me the righteousness of His own Son. He 'imparts' it to me. He makes it a part of me. He puts it into me ... there is a new seed of life 'implanted in me.' The seed is to grow and develop within us. It is to be accepted, not rejected. We are to provide an environment in which it will grow." **(Martyn Lloyd-Jones)**

He [Luther] saw that this righteousness of God is given through faith and that it is something which can be received immediately. **(Martyn Lloyd-Jones)**

To know about imputed righteousness, to know about imparted righteousness, to know that my relationship to God is based upon fact, not some faint hope or wish, but facts that are comforting and satisfying. It requires me to respond, to act, even though I am a fallible sinner incapable of attaining righteousness by myself. However, I can attain it through Christ Jesus and His grace. (**Robert B. Callahan, Sr.**)

God will show forth His righteousness in those who respond in faith and obedience. (**Robert B. Callahan, Sr.**)

The will to live a good and holy life, which Christ wants us to do, does not at all exclude the chief article in His teaching, namely, the free imputation of righteousness, by which through the kindness of forgiveness our duties are pleasing to God, although in themselves they deserve to be rejected as imperfect and impure. Therefore, believers are regarded as keeping His commandments when they apply themselves to them, though they be far distant from the mark. (**John Calvin**)

Righteousness means knowing and obeying God's commands, and conforming to His revealed will. Then follows: godliness, faith, love, patience, meekness. (**Author Unknown**).

Righteousness is obtained through faith, and resides in faith in Christ. The righteousness of the law must be given up and renounced, that you may be righteous through faith, and second, the righteousness of faith comes from God. It does not belong to man. (**John Calvin**)

Righteousness means being obedient to the will of God by exercising through faith, as Abraham did, the right ordering, right understanding, right living, and right relationships. It means accepting Christ as their leader and becoming a knowledgeable follower. (**Robert B. Callahan, Sr.**)

The Apostle [Paul] asserts that you cannot have morality without godliness. There are people who are concerned about morality, but they are not concerned about godliness and righteousness. There have been people who have said over the past eighty to eight-five years that morality is good. How you act and how you treat your neighbor is good, but we do need godliness, [they say]we do not believe in the supernatural, we do not believe in miracles, and we do not believe that Jesus Christ is the

Son of God. These people thought they could preserve morality without godliness. But you cannot! **(Martyn Lloyd-Jones)**

Sin is opposed to righteousness. Paul teaches explicitly that we were made righteous as a direct result of Christ having been made sin and assuming our sin. That is the only way. When talking of righteousness in this respect, we are describing something imputed or attributed to us. It is not one of our qualities, habits, or capabilities. It is the righteousness of Christ. **(Robert B. Callahan, Sr.)**

Paul understood from the law, the prophets, the psalmists, the apostles, and the teachings of the Master that righteousness is a gift to be added to day-by-day and year-by-year. But, there is a catch to this righteousness. Yes, it is a gift. But there is a condition attached to it. You are to use it. You are not to exchange it, you are not to throw it away, and you are not to hide it. You are to use it. **(Robert B. Callahan, Sr.)**

Men should be carefully warned that righteousness and salvation are obtained by Christ's death that we may become God's holy possession. **(John Calvin)**

30

SANCTIFICATION

He separated you by the Spirit to believe the truth (sanctification). You are not separated because you believe it, but so you can believe it! There is a great truth in this statement. The separation comes first, before obedience and believing the truth. **(Robert B. Callahan, Sr.)**

Sanctification is, in reality, what Oswald Chambers says, "Christ in you." He further states that "sanctification means" imparting "the Holy qualities of Jesus Christ." Notice the term used is imparting. This means giving or granting from one's abundance. It means transmitting to another. It is entirely different from either acquiring or imitating.

The sanctification process means that we yield ourselves to His will and that He imparts to us "His patience, His purity, and His Godliness" as Chambers says. When these qualities are imparted to us and we receive them willingly, then our character, conduct and conversation reflect His qualities. **(Oswald Chambers)**

There are heart Christians and there are nominal Christians. The heart Christians know the Lord Jesus Christ. **(Gil Green)**

No one is a believer who is not holy and no one is holy who is not a believer. **(William Temple)**

Christ expressly says that the truth by which God sanctifies His sons exists nowhere but in the Word. What is meant by the Word? Calvin notes that it is "the teaching of the Gospel, which the Apostles had already heard from the mouth of their Master and which they were afterwards to proclaim. **(John Calvin)**

It is important to begin thinking of our sins in terms of our relationship to God. How can we proceed through the process of sanctification without having a positive relationship with God and His Son Jesus Christ? The sooner we begin to think this way, the sooner we shall become more committed Christians. **(Robert B. Callahan, Sr.)**

The New Testament teaches that the importance of sanctification is not something you receive as an experience. Sanctification is not the result of one gift or occasion. It results from the truth of God working within us. Jesus said, *"I am the way, the truth and the life."* That truth is to work within us, if we are to experience sanctification. When the truth works within us we are in the light and no longer in darkness. **(Robert B. Callahan, Sr.)**

When we are members of Christ's body, we are the children of God, therefore, we are to conduct ourselves as His children. We are to put on the new man in truth and He is to govern our conduct and our activities. Remember, when we do this people are going to judge God, judge the Gospel, and judge Christ by what they see in us. It is an awesome thought! Of course, people are wrong to judge in that manner, but they do, and you cannot do anything about it. **(Robert B. Callahan, Sr.)**

Anyone desiring holiness of life must realize that it comes only through life in Christ and by the power of the Holy Spirit. You cannot be saved by faith without at the same time laying hold of Christ for sanctification, for holiness of life. Our faith opens the door to the heart, but it is the Saviour and the Holy Spirit who do the work of sanctification. **(Robert B. Callahan, Sr.)**

Justification is not the original cause of sanctification, but rather its constant grounds. Sanctification, in turn, is not just the consequence of justification but rather its living and continual effort in the concrete life of man. **(Otto Weber)**

When we are cornered or troubled, the Lord opens a way; when we are oppressed or perplexed He comes to our aid; when we are surrounded he strengthens and supports us; when we are in deep trouble He will support us and stay with us. He will not allow us to be destroyed or overwhelmed. (**Robert B. Callahan, Sr.**)

First, God's part and our part in this matter of sanctification. It is not all God's doing, whereby we are merely passive vessels waiting to be turned on or turned around. These verses are "the crossroads between God's sovereign work through grace and man's cooperative action through faith." (**Ruth Paxson**)

We have no right to pick and choose. God's way of salvation takes up the intellect, the heart (emotions), the will, the understanding, the sensibilities, the experience, the practice, everything, the whole man. (**Martyn Lloyd-Jones**)

Christ asks that the Father would first sanctify the disciples; that He would consecrate them entirely to Himself and defend them as His sacred property. (**John Calvin**)

Jesus prays that His Father will sanctify them through the truth. (**Martyn Lloyd-Jones**)

Where does the Bible start teaching about sanctification? Where is the emphasis? With the individual? That you can be happy and enjoy life? That you can overcome problems, defeats, and obstacles? Is that where sanctification begins? No! No! No! It begins with God. Not with you or me. It begins with the nature and character of God. (**Robert B. Callahan, Sr.**)

No root of bitterness, no system of wrath, no trace of anger, no echo of clamor, no slime of evil speaking, and no dregs of malice are to remain in a person, nor are they to be seen in one's conduct at any time or place. (**Ruth Paxson**)

God has chosen you to Himself, has sanctified you, and received you unto His love, on the condition that you shall be merciful. (**John Clavin**)

What about fruit trees?

> Did you ever notice that at first they are barren, then they get buds and flowers, the the fruit is pollinated, and it receives light.
> There are things within the fruit tree that develop, respond to the light and make them fertile. After this, the fruit begins to appear, it grows, develops, and matures.
> It does not happen suddenly, it takes time, nutrients, care pruning, spraying, picking. There is no such thing as instant fruit, nor are there instant Christians, nor immediate, mature members of Christ's body. (**Robert B. Callahan, Sr.**)

What truth is used to sanctify? The Word! What is the Word that sanctifies? Is it a special formula? Is it a special act? Is it administering a sacrament? Is it saying, I believe? Is it blindly accepting by faith? Is it trusting and obeying? No, it is not any one or all of these things. . . . It is the whole of Scripture. It is working with it, probing it, asking why, under-standing it, and applying it. (**Robert B. Callahan, Sr.**)

The teaching [preaching] of sanctification is to be based upon doctrine and understanding, accompanied by an exhortation to apply the doctrine in a logical manner. Lest we forget or ignore Scripture, sanctification is not the result of our own efforts, but requires God working within us through the Holy Spirit. . . . He does it by presenting the doctrine and urging the followers to work it out in detail and to apply it. This is contrary to the teaching that you can get it for nothing, that it is a gift, and that you have nothing to do. (**Robert B. Callahan, Sr.**)

Jesus prays that His Father will sanctify them through the truth. (**Martyn Lloyd-Jones**)

The work of sanctification is neither easy nor simple. It is a challenging task, because it means becoming Christ-like in our attitude and conduct. . . . It requires God working within us as we struggle within ourselves to please Him. (**Robert B. Callahan, Sr.**)

We need to be scrupulously careful about every detail of our conduct, for nothing is trivial or unimportant. Our manner of speech, fashion in clothes, companions in pleasure, use of time, choice of magazines and books, expenditure of money, are all indicative of the degree of supremacy of light over darkness in our lives. Strictest consistency in common things is obligatory, for we are taught to avoid every appearance of evil. We are to refrain from doing that which could give rise to scandal, and that which belies the sanctity of our life in Christ. (**Robert B. Callahan, Sr.**)

When a person begins to grow in Christ it does not mean the change will be immediate and complete. We should not be surprised by these things:

>A violent temper being changed to gentleness, or
>
>Selfishness expanding into generosity, or
>
>A suspicious nature becoming modest, or
>
>The proud person becoming humble, or
>
>The irresponsible becoming responsible.

These changes do not occur without encouragement, support, strength and knowledge which is available in Christ Jesus. There is always a lag time as evidenced in the parable of the father asking his two sons to work in the fields. (**Robert B. Callahan, Sr.**)

31

SATAN / DEVIL

For now in blood and battles was my youth,
And full of blood and battles is my age;
And I shall never end this life of blood.
(Matthew Arnold)

Such is Satan's enmity and envy against a Christian's joy and comfort, that he cannot but act to the utmost of his life to keep poor souls in doubt and darkness. Satan knows that assurance is a pearl of that price that will make the soul happy forever; he knows that assurance makes a Christian's wilderness to be a paradise; he knows that assurance begets in Christians that most noble and generous spirits; he knows that assurance is that which will make men strong to do exploits, to shake his tottering kingdom about his ears; and therefore he is very studious and industrious to keep souls from assurance, as he was to cast Adam out of Paradise. **(Thomas Brooks)**

There is an interesting dichotomy to consider:

> Satan can never rest and is always striving to darken or tarnish the pure doctrine of Christ, yet God wants our faith to be tried and tested by these very struggles. **(Robert B. Callahan, Sr.)**

Satan can never rest without striving to darken by his lies the pure doctrine of Christ, and God wants to try our faith with these struggles. **(John Calvin)**

When Satan cannot make a direct attack upon us, he deceives us by pretending that there is nothing wrong in our starting all sorts of speculations for the sake of finding out what the truth is. **(John Calvin)**

Satan strives to infect and corrupt (the purity of Scripture) by all sorts of errors. **(John Calvin)**

O, what need have we to study the Scriptures, our hearts, and Satan's wiles, that we may not bid this enemy welcome and all the while think it is Christ that is our guest. **(William Gurnall)**

Unbelief is always proud and a despiser of God; but does not always break out into open conflict with God. **(John Calvin)**

Take heed of him as a seducer. **(William Gurnall)**

The devil is not primarily our enemy, he is the enemy of God. It was against God that he lifted up himself, it was against God that he rebelled; and it is against God that he wages the conflict. He uses us in our ignorance and folly to attack God. It is God who made us, and God who redeemed us at a tremendous cost; and if the devil can defeat us he defeats God. **(Martyn Lloyd-Jones)**

There is nothing about us that the devil cannot take hold of. It is because it has happened to us, because it is ours, because it is we who have done it. And, he will take even the most glorious gift and will twist it in this subtle manner. He will so bring self into it that the whole thing will be ruined. **(Martyn Lloyd-Jones)**

The devil does not always appear ugly and foul and harsh and cruel. He can be most pleasant, affable, and ingratiating. Many are deceived by these changes. Affability is what most people mean by saintliness today. "So nice" they say, so pleasant. "I talked to the man and he was so kind." But the question is, what does he believe? The important question in this realm is not whether a man is nice or not. The question is, what is he saying? What does he say about the truth? "Ah, but he is so nice," people say, "He never says an unkind word about anyone." "Therefore he must be a wonderful Christian," says the believer who has not got his feet shod with the preparation of the Gospel of peace. (**Martyn Lloyd-Jones**)

There would be no evil in the world if there were no evil persons, there would be no evil human beings unless there were spiritual beings who entered into God's creation, tempted man and seduced him in the calamity of the Fall. (**Martyn Lloyd-Jones**)

Satan seized the opportunity to disturb the church; for He is the stone of offence, against whom all must stumble who do not keep to the right way which God has shown us. (**John Calvin**)

A devil touched, hate tipped tongue will go to any length of railing, slander, insult, and abuse in giving vent to anger. (**Ruth Paxson**)

The archenemy of Christ is attacking His body which the brethren are members. Therefore, no one is exempt from the conflict. God has no place for a spiritual pacifist. (**Ruth Paxson**)

The power of the devil is very definitely acknowledged in Scripture, so, for us to deny it when God admits it is sheer folly. In fact, men are held captive by the power of Satan until delivered from it by the power of the Saviour. (**Robert B. Callahan, Sr.**)

O' the insight and positive approach that Calvin provides in the time of trouble. He had learned from his encounters with Satan and Satan's minions that he would face continuous assaults as he served the Lord Jesus. He came to the realization that Jesus was not only his refuge, but his strength, his wisdom, and his armor. Therefore, Paul knew [we should know] in whom he trusted, the Lord Jesus Christ. May we be able to say with the Apostle Paul, *Nay, in all these things we are more than conquerors through him that loved us* [Rom. 8:37]. (**Robert B. Callahan, Sr.**)

Paul says the real problem is the struggle against the principalities and powers. Therefore the inner man needs to be strengthened, because this power that confronts him is great, subtle, devious, and cunning. The devil is not only an accuser, he is an adversary, and as an adversary he can turn himself into an angel of light. . . . He can quote Scripture, reason, rationalize, present arguments and cases, and appear to describe or discuss a truth, but he will lead you astray. **(Martyn Lloyd-Jones)**

The devil makes a special effort to attack the inner man. Unfortunately, there is much emphasis on the sins of the flesh and relatively little attention focused on the lusts of the mind and heart. Consequently, people are not cognizant of the subtleties or attacks that can be made on the inner man by various means and methods.. The evil one may ignore the outward person and concentrate on the inner one. Solomon proclaims a great truth when he says,
. [Prov. 4:23] **(Author Unknown)**

Thus at every touch of temptation we should rouse ourselves and quickly put on our armor to drive back Satan's attacks. **(John Calvin)**

You can be sure of one thing, the devil knows human nature. He knows how self thinks and acts. How a person takes pride in the gifts he or she has received such as intellect, perception, understanding, knowledge. **(Robert B. Callahan, Sr.)**

There was a philosopher in England who lived prior to, during and for a while after World War II. He had been an atheist, an unbeliever. However, he came to believe in the fact of God. Why? Because he became convinced that the second war occurred due to the principle of evil at work and that the Bible was right about this fact. He could not explain the war except that there was a devilish, evil power at work. **(Robert B. Callahan, Sr.)**

It occurs, as Otto Weber says, "wherever the church in its proclamation makes a given or inherited human, self-understanding into the criterion of the Word."

> How does this happen? As Weber continues, "Invariably... with the best of intentions:
> - To mitigate the strangeness of the proclaimed Word,
> - To make it easier for the listener to find access to the Word, and
> - To make it possible for the believer to exist in his "world."

And, to make the word more palatable, more in conformity to the world and far less demanding.

The Word may be presented in such a way as to confirm worldviews and to reflect them. The teachings become focused on man, his existence, his importance, his creatureliness, his capabilities, his ideas and beliefs. The focus is not upon God, the creator, the Giver of Life, nor upon the Lord Jesus Christ as man's redeemer and strength.

The Word will be presented in such a way that it does not appear to contradict Scripture. As a matter of fact, it may even use Scripture and appear to be pious, moral or rational, when in reality it is distorting the truth as it is in Christ.

This is one of the *"wiles of the devil."* He wants us to fall, not to stand. One thing needs to be clarified and realized. The devil is not a principle, but a person.
(Otto Weber)

There is no length to which Satan will not go to dislodge the saint from his faith position in Christ. **(Ruth Paxson)**

The problem is that . . . people do not have a clear understanding of the Christian faith. They have an utterly inadequate notion of what Christianity means. Their idea of Christianity was or is: Believe in Christ and you will never have another trouble or problem; God will bless you, nothing will ever go wrong with you. **(Martyn Lloyd-Jones)**

Observe the fallacy of Satan's argument, which discovered, will help thee to answer his cavil. **(William Gurnall)**

Thus at every touch of temptation we should rouse ourselves and quickly put on our armor to drive back Satan's attacks. **(John Calvin)**

Yes, the devil is a formidable foe. Yes, false teachings, and devious methods are employed.

But, we are to turn to the Lord, obey His commandments, become knowledgeable, and grasp the strength available from the Lord Jesus to fight against this subtle foe and to defeat him by God's grace, power, and might.

This requires: obtaining the proper knowledge about God and His teachings; exerting the necessary effort in learning how to use God's armor; and becoming proficient in using it to repel Satan's attacks as we serve the Lord Jesus day in and day out. (**Robert B. Callahan, Sr.**)

Make no mistake, the devil, or the evil one, is perfectly content when people are not changed by the power of the gospel and the Holy Spirit. He is very satisfied when church members hear moral essays or have the gospel presented in a theoretical way, or appeals are made for people to be decent, law abiding citizens. (**Robert B. Callahan, Sr.**)

We need to obtain a clear understanding of what the Apostle [Paul] teaches here about the devil and the principalities and powers, the world rulers of this darkness, the wicked spirits in the heavenlies. (**Martyn Lloyd-Jones**)

How true this is! Can you imagine that the General Assembly would expunge the hymns, Onward Christian Soldiers, the Old Rugged Cross and others, because they are too war-like? They don't realize we are in a war with Satan and all his evil forces. They don't understand what Scripture teaches. They are ignorant. (**Robert B. Callahan, Sr.**)

Paul declares that faith which rests upon the Word of God stands unshaken against all the attacks of Satan. (**John Calvin**)

You are in a very difficult world, a sinful world, a world that is dominated by the devil and his cohorts. These principalities and powers! It tells you that you will often find it difficult just to stand on your feet at all. Indeed you will need the whole armor of God; you will need to be "strengthened" with might by his Spirit in the inner man; you will need to be *"strong in the Lord, and in the power of his might."* Then you will be able to stand, but only then. 'Quit you like men; be strong!' " (**Martyn Lloyd-Jones**)

He says to himself, I have been fighting ever since I have become a Christian; and I am still fighting. Is there no end to it? That means that the devil is attacking and trying to get him to feel that the whole thing is vain and useless. **(Martyn Lloyd-Jones)**

We have seen that Satan comes to us first as a liar and deceiver, so we can understand why God provides first of all the girdle of truth for our protection. Christ, the truth and the true God, is our armor against the attacks of Satan, the liar and deceiver. **(Robert B. Callahan, Sr.)**

God has told us we would have temptations, trials, testings, so we must be prepared to stand the strain of the slippery paths of temptation and the stony hills of adversity and affliction . . . as we walk through this disordered world there are a thousand things to bruise and wound us . . . . The battle with Satan continues throughout our lives, and as good soldiers of Christ, we are to use the whole armor of God in our fight against Satan and his evil forces. **(Ruth Paxson)**

People are the way they are and the world is as it is because of their listening and responding to the devil. The devil is so powerful that he is able to persuade people that he is not dominating them, guiding them, or leading them.

Jesus called him the prince of this world;
> He was an angel created by God,
> He stood up against God,
> He hates God,
> He wants to ruin God's world,
> He beguiled Eve and Adam, and
> He dominates the life of man.
> **(Robert B. Callahan, Sr.)**

Some interpreters claim that righteousness can be interpreted as moral rectitude, or integrity, or being a just and good person. These traits may be respected by certain people. Each one is desirable, but it is inadequate when confronted by the *"wiles of the devil,"* when wrestling against flesh and blood, principalities, powers, rulers of darkness, and spiritual wickedness. Human traits are inadequate in the war against Satan and can not be depended upon. **(Robert B. Callahan, Sr.)**

As I walk in the commandments and ordinances of the Lord, why do I need the breastplate of righteousness? To keep things from harming me and my relationship to God. Such things as: spiritual depression; trials and tribulations; distractions and discouragement; entanglements that keep us from the word of God; perplexities, despair and persecution; and questioning the authority of Christ. Each of these things can happen and beset the saints and faithful within the church as well as when we venture into the secular environment. These things can overwhelm us, especially when we think we have been working and have been obedient. The devil will appeal to us. He will tempt us, he will beguile us.

When these things happen we are required to do a very difficult thing. We are to "rest in the Lord and wait patiently for Him." When we do this, we are in a state of preparedness. We have done the things we are to do as our Scripture says, *"having put on the breastplate of righteousness."* We are to remember who we are and our calling. **(Robert B. Callahan, Sr.)**

32

SELF

The Apostle wants us to realize that the primary obstacle to a successful, positive relationship with the Lord Jesus Christ is the same one that has a negative impact on a successful marriage, namely self and all its derivatives and manifestations. Self wants things for itself. One of the unfortunate things about this is that the desires of self are more evident in others, at least to ourselves, than they are in our own being. We have that wonderful dangerous trait of rationalization. It works most effectively and ingeniously when self is involved. Think about it, observe yourself and see how deceptively it works. (**Robert B. Callahan, Sr.**)

You don't say that to a principle, you say that to a person, to a being. If you deny that the devil is a person then you are denying that the Lord dealt with him in that manner. You are establishing yourself in a position of knowledge and understanding that is above and beyond the Lord Jesus. When you do that you are involved in the whole question of revelation and of authority. (**Martyn Lloyd-Jones**)

When men abandon themselves to unrestrained license they remove all barriers between good and evil, pleasing and displeasing God, and righteousness and unrighteousness. (**John Calvin**)

Anyone . . . ought to grow with time . . . (it) is inexcusable if he remains forever a child. (**John Calvin**)

Christ, by exercising His power toward you in my teaching, has proved that He speaks through my mouth so that there is no excuse for your ignorance. **(John Calvin)**

How foolish it is to wish to measure God's immensity by our measure. **(John Calvin)**

Self is everything, nothing matters but self. I must have what I want, when I want it, and the more the better. **(Martyn Lloyd-Jones)**

For when once men have given themselves the freedom to command, they demand a strict observance of their laws and will not bear the least letter of the law to be left out either by contempt or oversight. The world is impatient of legitimate rule and especially stubborn against bearing the yoke of God. Yet it will quickly and willingly ensnare itself in empty traditions; nay, many seem to desire such slavery. And so the worship of God is vitiated, for its principle and head is obedience. The authority of men is preferred to His rule. **(John Calvin)**

Throughout the Bible it is clear that self is the outstanding problem in human life. [Further], as you read the Old Testament and the New there is no problem that raises its head more frequently than this horrible, terrible problem of self, whether seen in individuals, or groups, or nations. What havoc this whole problem of self has caused in the long history of the human race. **(Martyn Lloyd-Jones)**

The essential thing is my personal relationship to Jesus Christ–that I may know him. To fulfill God's design means, complete abandonment to Him. Whenever I want things for myself, the relationship is distorted. It will be a big humiliation to realize that I have not been concerned about realizing Jesus Christ, but only about realizing what He has done for me. **(Oswald Chambers)**

A proud heart and a lofty mountain are never fruitful. **(William Gurnall)**

There is a sense in which morality is a very insulting thing to a human being, it is only interested in my behavior. **(Martyn Lloyd-Jones)**

We fail to recognize God in that we are not willing to accept that he is good to us. We fail to recognize ourselves in that we are not willing to accept [the truth] that we should submit ourselves to him. **(Otto Weber)**

If in this frail and transitory life God acts so powerfully . . . , how absurd it is to want to measure by the apprehension of our own mind His secret work in the heavenly and supernatural life and believe no more than we can see! **(John Calvin)**

Religious excitement originating by direct contact with God will always enlarge and exalt our conception of God's greatness, and will deepen our sense of dependence on Him . . . , but as emotion becomes more intense and as our conceptions of the Christian life become more and more glorious, the infinite greatness of God's righteousness and power and grace will inspire us with deeper wonder and awe. On the other hand, religious excitement created by the imagination, though it may suggest lofty ideas of moral and spiritual perfection, and inspire a vehement and chivalrous desire to translate these ideas into conduct, will leave us with a new sense of our own greatness rather than a new sense of the greatness of God. **(R.W. Dale)**

From avarice there can come the greatest evil of all–apostasy from the faith. **(John Calvin)**

Intellectual lethargy is probably the greatest sin of many members of the community of believers today. Too many are content to recount their early experiences, with their primary level of learning, or to base everything on their carnal knowledge. They remain where they began. **(Robert B. Callahan, Sr.)**

The teachings of God as found in the Scriptures pay us a wonderful compliment. They do not treat us as children or as "nincompoops." They reason with us, they appeal to our understanding, if we will keep an open mind and not let self get in the way. The teaching is reasoned out. This is the process for imparting holiness and sanctification. We should be thankful for it. **(Robert B. Callahan, Sr.)**

Pride exhibits itself in many ways. We can be oversensitive or insensitive. Pride leads to envy, jealousy, and carrying grudges. Pride is no respecter of persons. One thing is certain about pride, it spoils God's handiwork. **(Robert B. Callahan, Sr.)**

Probably, the greatest hindrance to accepting and realizing this fact is our lack of knowledge about God and His Son.

> It is not knowing Him as we should.
> It is from having other ambitions.
> It is from allowing the old self to get in the way.
> **(Robert B. Callahan, Sr.)**

We can plainly see how great is the blindness of the human mind, which surrounded by light, perceives nothing. For it is true that the world is like a theatre in which the Lord shows to us a striking spectacle of His glory. However, when such a sight lies open before our eyes, we are quite blind, not because the revelation is obscure, but because we are alienated in mind, meaning that not only the will but also the power for this activity fails us. For notwithstanding that God shows Himself openly, yet it is only by the eye of faith that we can look at Him, bearing in mind that we receive only a slight inkling as to His divine nature, but enough to put us in the position of being without excuse. **(John Calvin)**

If we claim (or profess) that we are church members (or go to church) having fellowship with God, yet walk in darkness (or according to the ways of the world), then we are liars in whom there is no truth. **(Martyn Lloyd-Jones)**

We focus our eyeballs inwardly, instead of outwardly. **(Chuck Swindoll)**

Paul says, *"Because the carnal mind is enmity against God, for it is not subject to the law of God, neither indeed can be."* **(Rom 8:7)**

Few have courage and resolution to grapple with the difficulties that meet them in the way to their happiness. **(William Gurnall)**

There is nothing about us that the devil cannot take hold of. It is because it has happened to us, because it is ours, because it is we who have done it. And, he will take even the most glorious gift and will twist it in this subtle manner. He will so bring self into it that the whole thing will be ruined. **(Martyn Lloyd-Jones)**

"NONE OF SELF AND ALL OF THEE"

Oh, the bitter shame and sorrow
That a time could ever be
When I let the Saviour's pity
Plead in vain, and proudly answered,
"All of self and none of Thee."

Yet He found me; I beheld Him
Bleeding on the accursed tree;
Heard Him pray, "Forgive them, Father;"
And my wistful heart said faintly,
"Some of self and some of Thee."

Day by day, His tender mercy,
Healing, helping, full and free,
Sweet and strong, and, oh, so patient,
Brought me lower, while I whispered,
"Less of self and more of Thee."

Higher than the highest heavens,
Deeper than the deepest sea,
Lord, Thy love at last has conquered;
Grant me now my soul's desire,
"None of self and all of Thee."
(Theodore Monod)

The idea of enmity against God is difficult for some to accept. We have all heard people say, "I know someone who is not a Christian or an active Christian but they believe in God." They really don't. They believe in their own ideas, in the figment of their imaginations. They do not believe in God the Father of our Lord Jesus Christ. **(Robert B. Callahan, Sr.)**

The characteristics of corrupt communications . . . are marked by excesses and lack of self-control. It is when people talk too much and talk without thinking . . . . Their conversations are usually an expression of self. It is self-centered, it focuses on self, it is selfish, and it presents self first and foremost. **(Robert B. Callahan, Sr.)**

33

SIN / SINNER

Intellectual lethargy is probably the greatest sin of many members of the community of believers today. Too many are content to recount their early experiences, with their primary level of learning, or to base everything on their carnal knowledge. They remain where they began. **(Robert B. Callahan, Sr.)**

The unbelieving may be satisfied with their own acuteness, and may even seem to others to be wise and prudent, yet, the Spirit of God condemns them for their folly, in order that we may know that, apart from God, we cannot be really wise, as without Him there is nothing firm. **(John Calvin)**

Truly and sincerely fear God and desire to submit to His righteousness. However, the ungodly, those who have an evil conscience, those who do not fear God, and worship Him, they are not heard when they do call upon God. **(John Calvin)**

The Apostle John wants us to know that sin is evident and that it takes its toll in the community. He wants the faithful believers in Christ 'to beware of sin and to encourage them to repel the assaults of Satan.' **(John Calvin)**

Believers particularly . . . cannot progress in the Gospel until first they have been humbled, and this cannot happen until they are aware of their sins. **(John Calvin)**

When Christ talks about sin, He ties it deliberately to the statement, *"Of sin, because they believe not on me."* (**Jn 16:9**) Sin and the lack of belief go hand in hand. (**Robert B. Callahan, Sr.**)

Although God's power delivers us from sin and its power, it does not deliver us from sin's presence. That is a very important distinction. Even though we put off the old man, the temptations of the flesh and mind still are with us. (**Robert B. Callahan, Sr.**)

Sin is hostility toward the grace of God. (**Otto Weber**)

What is a sinner? It is someone who does no live to glorify God, who does not live according to God's will, who does not learn God's commandments and seek to obey them. It is someone who has not been living to serve the Lord seven days a week, fifty-two weeks a year, who puts himself or herself first and foremost, and lives to please himself or herself, not others. (**Robert B. Callahan, Sr.**)

We are to understand and appreciate what God has done through his grace in delivering us from such a life (alienated from God). There is an old maxim that says those who have the deepest understanding of sin and what it does are those who have the greatest understanding and appreciation of God's love, grace, mercy, and kindness. (**Martyn Lloyd-Jones**)

Wherever there is a departure from God there is a consequent deterioration in ethics and morals, and the breakdown in the latter is always gauged by the depth and degree of that in the former. The further one goes from God, the nearer he comes to Satan. The old Adamic nature remains unchanged . . . down through the centuries and left to itself it will wallow in the deepest mire of sin. If one needs proof of this he needs only to read the pages of modern literature, where the very sins mentioned in [Eph. 5:3–5] are pictured with appalling frankness; and often-times the writer is advocating a personal liberty, which is nothing less than free license to lust. (**Ruth Paxson**)

Our sins do not prevent us from pleasing Him (God) since we have been cleansed by the blood of Christ. It is the cleansing power of Christ's blood that makes us acceptable to God. **(Robert B. Callahan, Sr.)**

The sinner walks as *fools,* but the saint walks as *wise.* **(Ruth Paxson)**

They will receive punishment appropriate for their ungodliness. **(John Calvin)**

If we claim (profess) that we are church members having fellowship with God, yet walk in darkness (according to the ways of the world), then we are liars in whom there is no truth. **(Martyn Lloyd-Jones)**

While man is in sin, and while, as a result of that, he is always primarily and essentially selfish and self-centered, there will of necessity be tensions in different relationships. **(Martyn Lloyd-Jones)**

Sin and righteousness are so opposed to one another that anyone who devotes himself to the one must leave the other. **(John Calvin)**

When a person is a servant of sin, he is cutoff from righteousness. Conversely, when he seeks after righteousness, then he will be delivered from sin. **(Robert B. Callahan, Sr.)**

The great enemy of the life of faith in God is not sin, but the good which is not good enough. The good is always the enemy of the best. **(Oswald Chambers)**

The characteristics of individuality are independence and self-assertiveness. It is the continual assertion of individuality that hinders our spiritual life more than anything else. Individuality never can believe. Personality cannot help believing. **(Oswald Chamber)**

Where there is irreverence for the divine law the vision of God becomes fainter; as the vision of God becomes fainter the restraints of the Divine righteousness are lessened, irreverence and disobedience become more and more flagrant and at last the vision of God is lost altogether. **(R.W. Dale)**

Behold, the Lord's hand is not shortened, that it cannot save; neither his ear heavy, that it cannot hear: But your iniquities have separated between you and your God, and your sins have hid his face from you, that he will not hear. **(Isaiah 59:1–2)**

Love not the world, neither the things that are in the world. If any man love the world the love of the Father is not in Him. For all that is in the world, the lust of the flesh, and the lust of the eyes, and the pride of life, is not of the Father, but is of the world. **(I Jn 2:15–16)**

Contrast this today with the people outside Christ's Body. They "are not only in darkness, they are darkness; they do not know God, and the more they talk, the more they express their ignorance." **(Martyn Lloyd-Jones)**

There are others who wrestle with sin, but they do not hate it. Actually, they are favorably disposed to it. They do not consider the life of sin to be their enemy. These wrestle in jest, and not in earnest; the wounds they give sin one day, are healed by the next. **(William Gurnall)**

From avarice there can come the greatest evil of all–apostasy from the faith. **(John Calvin)**

Sin is hostility toward the grace of God. **(Otto Weber)**

The only way the love of sin can be quenched is to replace it with another love; the love of Christ. **(Robert B. Callahan, Sr.)**

As nations and, peoples in supposed 'wisdom' have turned their backs upon God the Creator, they have always become fools. **(Martyn Lloyd-Jones)**

Thus at every touch of temptation we should rouse ourselves and quickly put on our armor to drive back Satan's attacks **(John Calvin)**

A person cannot have a true conception of redemption unless he or she knows the Doctrine of Sin as presented in the Bible. If we do not know the Doctrine of Sin then we have vague ideas about redemption. **(Robert B. Callahan, Sr.)**

According to the Bible the world is always against God. (**Robert B. Callahan, Sr.**)

We cannot understand Calvary's Hill unless we know the Doctrine of Sin. What Christ did on the Cross cannot really be understood apart it. People have vague or false ideas about Jesus' death and that it is due to sin. Further, they do not like the idea of substitution or the Doctrine of Penal Suffering. They cannot bring themselves to start with man in sin. What we are discussing are the great truths of the Christian Faith and we cannot really understand them apart from man in sin. That is you and me! (**Robert B. Callahan, Sr.**)

Men mock God and themselves by the fruits of their unbelief. They add to this their pride, because unbelievers despise the Mediator's grace and throw themselves into the presence of God. (**John Calvin**)

The children of disobedience means according to Hebrew custom the obstinate. Unbelief is always accompanied by disobedience. It is the source and mother of all stubbornness. (**John Calvin**)

There is nothing more important to understand than the Doctrine of the Fall, man in sin; it is the key to the whole Bible! (**Martyn Lloyd-Jones**)

The fruit of the lips reveals the quality of the tree. Bad language and foul talk defile the whole man and manifest his corruption. (**Markus Barth**)

Sin is the cause of enmity between God and ourselves, between man and man. We can never be in God's favor until our sinful condition has been abolished. This was done on the Cross *"by the blood of Christ"* where He and He alone was able to achieve the ultimate victory in *"Having slain* (put to death) *the enmity thereby."* (**Robert B. Callahan, Sr.**)

The Pharisees were greater sinners than the Publicans. Why? Because they were self-satisfied, self-sufficient, and did not feel any need for the grace of God. (**Robert B. Callahan, Sr.**)

Without the shedding of blood, there is no remission of sins. It is that which enables us to become new creatures in Christ. (**Robert B. Callahan, Sr.**)

Sin and deceit always offer the one thing they can never give — satisfaction! (**Robert B. Callahan, Sr.**)

Sin is hostility toward the grace of God. (**Otto Weber**)

So what do we find, what do we see, what can we learn about the individual in sin?

- His mind is darkened,
- There is a veil of sin and unbelief,
- His mind and the ways of the world control him,
- His heart is wicked, deceitful, proud, and implacable,
- He is at enmity with God,
- It is not merely someone who does not abide by acceptable moral codes, who does not do what they should do and vice versa. It is someone: who does not live to the glory of God or to glorify God; who does not live to do God's will; and who does not learn God's commandments and seek to obey them.
- Further, it is someone: who realizes that he or she has not been living for the great objective of serving the Lord seven days a week, fifty-two (52) weeks a year; who puts himself or herself first and foremost; and who lives to please themselves not others.
- Yea, he even hates God,
- He is opposed to God, and
- He puts himself first.

   (**Robert B. Callahan, Sr.**)

What then is a sinner?

The Doctrine of Sin reveals that our troubles are due to disobedience, that man deliberately rebels against God. Why does he? Because of self-love, ego, self-assertion, and the desire to be a god. (**Robert B. Callahan, Sr.**)

He (Jesus) spoke of the state of sin because he realized the hearers needed God. He did not count their self-righteousness as sin, but condemned it for its self-centered confidence, arrogance, and lack of compassion. Jesus turned upside down the idea that sinners are a separated people. He made people realize that everyone is a sinner. He said to the multitude, *"Even so ye also outwardly appear righteous unto men, but within ye are full of hypocrisy and iniquity* (lawlessness)." **(Mt 23:28) (Robert B. Callahan, Sr.)**

God has stated the destiny of those who prefer to remain in the kingdom of darkness and to practice the works of darkness, and further comment seems unnecessary. God's attitude towards sin remains inflexible. God and sin can never fellowship together. His love and grace ever go out to the sinner; but he has only hatred and wrath toward the sin. **(Ruth Paxson)**

Sin is deceitful! How does it deceive? First, it always flatters us. It appeals to our egos, to our pride, to our self-centeredness, and to building ourselves up while tearing others down. It preys on the vanity of our minds by exalting our being position, status and power. This has been true since the time of Adam and Eve. **(Robert B. Callahan, Sr.)**

34

THE CHURCH

The Church is not above the scriptures. The standard by which you judge even the Church is the scriptures. (**Martyn Lloyd-Jones**)

The Community is related to its Lord and Head in a one-sidedly determined unity: it is not its own lord or its own head. Because Jesus Christ is its Lord and Head, it lives not its own life, but His life. (**Otto Weber**)

Martyn Lloyd-Jones asks a very penetrating question, "Can you see your church as she is today in the New Testament?" This is a question that we must ask? However, if we ask it, then we must be prepared to learn what the New Testament has to say. We must be able to distinguish between the teachings of Christ and the pronouncements of men. (**Martyn Lloyd-Jones**)

Concludes with wonder at the spiritual union between Christ and the Church. For he exclaims that this is a great mystery. (**John Calvin**)

A man once said when discussing miracles that when the church could say–'Silver and gold have I none, it could say in the name of Jesus Christ of Nazareth, rise up and walk.' Today the church has silver and gold, it has become large and powerful, it has lobbyists, but it seems to have forgotten holiness. (**Robert B. Callahan, Sr.**)

God still works through the Church; the church is His own creation. (**Martyn Lloyd-Jones**)

There is a significant observation to make about the church throughout the past 2,000 years. Where the gospel is proclaimed, as it was in the first century, where people apply themselves to hearing it, that is where the living Christ is present, and where the true church will be found. **(Robert B. Callahan, Sr.)**

What is the chief function of the Church, as the body of Christ? It is to open the Word, expound upon Scripture, and through the Holy Spirit enable people to learn, grow, and become new creatures in Christ, by God's grace. **(Robert B. Callahan, Sr.)**

Christ's love for the Church is such that it incorporates the will, the power, the patience, the understanding, the strength, the wisdom, and the knowledge to make her perfect. His love is a working love. It feeds, it waters, it nourishes the Church. Also, His love rebukes, chastises and even scourges the Church when it is necessary. Christ loves the Church for her sake, not His. **(Robert B. Callahan, Sr.)**

God chooses to dwell in a pure church with a pure body of believers, pure in doctrine, and pure in life. But let's not forget, His Son came to save sinners that we may have fellowship with Him and the Father *now* and forevermore. In that holy fellowship we are given the clothing of righteousness. **(Robert B. Callahan, Sr.)**

Without the presence of the Lord Jesus Christ the church is nothing. And I repeat: it is nothing. **(Robert B. Callahan, Sr.)**

The primary task of the church is to preach the gospel, to evangelize, and to bring people to a knowledge of God, to reach people under the dominion of sin, and to strengthen those who are not knowledgeable in the ways of the Lord. **(Robert B. Callahan, Sr.)**

What has been required of most church members during much of the 20th Century and into the 21st Century?
- Make a profession of faith;
- Join the church;
- Attend services on Sundays;

- Let the fulltime minister take care of most matters, and
- Perform worldly tasks according to human standards.

What does the Apostle say to the members of Christ's body? Wherever you go, whatever you do, your standard of conduct is to be the Lord Jesus Christ and your relationship to Him. Therefore, if that is the standard, you must learn about Him, you must assimilate His teachings, and above all you must come to know Him. (**Robert B. Callahan, Sr.**)

We walk as pilgrims in an unregenerate world.... We walk as Christians in the midst of an apostate Church, wherein the world, the flesh, and the devil have been allowed great liberty in dictating its plans and in the control of its programs. In no period of church history was God's exhortation, *See then* (Therefore) *that ye walk circumspectly* (carefully), *not as fools, but as wise* [**Eph. 5:5**] more needed than today. (**Ruth Paxson**)

Unfortunately, too often in today's world the control of the church at various levels is in the hands of those who are wise in the ways of the world and strangers to the purposes of God revealed in Christ Jesus. The ways of the world are adopted and espoused, while the ways of the Lord are ignored or relegated to a secondary position. (**Robert B. Callahan, Sr.**)

The most important factor in the life of the community of believers, more important than any so-called accomplishments or achievements that may be identified, is that the Christian community in its speaking, acting and serving points beyond itself. It must always point to the centrality of Christ. It must continually point to Christ as its Lord, Head, and Shepherd, to the obedient servant with the crown of thorns going to Calvary's Hill and shedding His blood. All other activities, proclamations, and urgings pale in comparison to what Christ did. We are *in Christ* and we are members of the community. Therefore, our obedience is to be to God's will in accordance with Christ's teachings and His life. (**Robert B. Callahan, Sr.**)

The community of believers can have unity with Jesus Christ only through its dependence upon Him and its obedience to Him. The community is a company of people under human direction. It does not have all the good or better people; it does not have all the activists or doers of good deeds; or people who accomplish great things; but it contains people who have a relationship with the Lord Jesus Christ and are dependent upon Him. (**Robert B. Callahan, Sr.**)

There is nothing magical about adding to the church rolls. It is doing what the early church did: proclaim the Gospel; prick (stab) their hearts; teach doctrine; repent and be baptized; realize the presence of the living God; receive the gift of the Holy Spirit; and praise God for all His blessings and gifts. (**Robert B. Callahan, Sr.**)

Christ is the one and only foundation of the church. (**John Calvin**)

35

WISDOM

We must learn from the whole of life, because the truly wise man is the one who knows how far short he comes of any complete understanding. **(John Calvin)**

This strikes at the heart of the matter that God is wiser than we are. That is why Paul calls them the *"unsearchable riches of Christ."* By this he means that although they exceed our ability to grasp them, they deserve our reverence and admiration. Therefore, our rashness, or lack of forethought, or impetuousness must be suppressed when God's divine foreknowledge is revealed. **(Robert B. Callahan, Sr.)**

A review of history books, the Old Testament, Romans 1:18–32, the Greek philosophers, and, the Decline and Fall of the Roman Empire will reveal that "As nations, and peoples in supposed 'wisdom' have turned their backs upon God the Creator, they have always become fools." **(Martyn Lloyd-Jones)**

The lusts of the flesh divide, the fruit of the Spirit unites. **(Robert B. Callahan, Sr.)**

36

WORD OF GOD

Calvin states that Jesus is praying to God saying, "It is for thee to protect those who are hated by the world because of the word." **(John Calvin)**

The same Word of God that offers us pardon, calls us at the same time to repentance. **(John Calvin)**

The Lord in no way measures his precepts according to our strength, or the power of free will, nor does he instruct us in our duty, so that we may place reliance on our own powers and prepare ourselves to render obedience. Rather, the precepts which he gives us require the assistance of His grace to stimulate us to an assiduous desire for prayer . . . It is only when we embrace what we are taught calmly, gladly and with one mind, that we are really prepared for *faith*. **(John Calvin)**

Calvin says that the Apostle Paul in writing to Timothy (II Tim 3:16) "commends the scripture because of its authority, and then because of the profit that comes from it. To assert its authority he teaches that it is inspired of God . . . and we know that God has spoken to us and are fully convinced that the prophets did not speak of themselves." **(John Calvin)**

What we most need to know about God can come only from God, and it does come through God's self-disclosure in the incarnate Word and the written Word; . . . furthermore, that self-disclosure is typically couched in terms accommodated to the limits of human capacity. **(Roland Frye)**

When you think about authority, truth, the Word, and yourself it is easy to succumb to the *"wiles of the devil"* and to say: What difference does it make; why put forth the effort; why bother? Think of Martin Luther. Suppose he had listened to the peer pressure. It does make a difference in what we believe, where we stand. We are to stand, as W.E. Gladstone calls it, on "The impregnable Rock of Scripture." (**Robert B. Callahan, Sr.**)

What is the Holy Spirit telling us? That the full light of the Gospel should have a positive impact upon our faith, beliefs, attitudes, actions, and practices. "A tiny spark of light led them to heaven, but now that the sun of righteousness shines on us what excuse shall we offer if we still hold to the earth or the things of the world?" (**John Calvin**)

The truth as it is used by Paul, is the objective truth which I possess in a subjective manner. (**M. Lloyd-Jones**)

Nothing (is) more abused than the word. And why? Because men come to it with unsound and unsanctified hearts. (**William Gurnall**)

Christ expressly says that the truth by which God sanctifies His sons exists nowhere but in the Word. What is meant by the Word? Calvin notes that it is "the teaching of the Gospel, which the Apostles had already heard from the mouth of their Master and which they were afterwards to proclaim." (**John Calvin**)

The dynamic, fermentative, life changing power of His gospel. (**Lloyd Ogilvie**)

This will require of us a constant, systematic study of God's word, that our sword may be easily and quickly unsheathed, and that just the needed part of it may be used at the right time and in the right way. (**Ruth Paxson**)

Take up the sword which the spirit Himself provides for you, that is to say, the Word of God; in other words the Scriptures, the Bible. (**Martyn Lloyd-Jones**)

The Word and the Holy Spirit worked amongst the people. They responded in faith. They began applying the teachings of Scripture. **(Robert B. Callahan, Sr.)**

Any teaching that detracts from, or minimizes, the Lord Jesus Christ as the Son of God and our Lord and Saviour is not of the Word, but is of *"the wiles of the devil."* **(Robert B. Callahan, Sr.)**

The righteousness of God is revealed from faith to faith, from the faith of one believer to the faith of another, but the wrath of God is revealed from heaven. The Holy Spirit has bestowed upon preachers and teachers the ability to tell people of God's grace, to proclaim the Gospel, and to communicate the faith, but the wrath is from heaven, therefore, it is to be proclaimed by preachers and teachers. When considering God's Word, bear in mind, it is a privilege to announce faith and righteousness, but it is a duty to announce wrath and unrighteousness. **(Robert B. Callahan, Sr.)**

The sword is God's own utterance given to us in His written Word, inspired by the Spirit, revealed to us by the Spirit **(Eph 1:17–18)**, used by the Spirit in us to sanctify and cleanse, **(Eph. 5:20)** and then wielded by the Spirit through us to defeat the devil. **(Eph. 6:17) (Ruth Paxson)**

Nothing is more abused than the word. And why? Because men come to it with unsound and unsanctified hearts. **(William Gurnall)**

Think of this: if the Bible is not acknowledged as the one and only authority, then *every wind of doctrine* is permissible. And if that is the case, then there is no Christian faith, and consequently no salvation. **(Robert B. Callahan, Sr.)**

We should pause, contemplate, examine and digest. We should become connoisseurs of Scripture. If we will, it will allow us to avoid being content with a knowledge of the "letters of the Scriptures," and motivate us to discover the principles and doctrines in the Bible. We are called to examine and realize the riches contained in the individual statements. **(Robert B. Callahan, Sr.)**

Preachers and teachers for the most part wish to present the pleasant accounts and teachings of Scripture, and to overstress the love of God, but that is not according to the divine revelation of God presented in the Gospel. We, the teachers and pastors, have no right to interpose our choices and priorities over divine revelation. (**Robert B. Callahan, Sr.**)

Paul does not boast in words, but proves that Christ speaks through him. He convinces the Corinthians that they should listen to him and to his claims. When it becomes clear that it is God's Word being proclaimed, then what Paul says holds true: that if people do not believe, then they are disbelieving God. This is true of preachers and teachers. (**Robert B. Callahan, Sr.**)

The Scripture being considered is very clear and says, truth is defined and error is condemned. (**Martyn Lloyd-Jones**)

Jesus Christ as attested to us in Holy Scripture is the one Word of God whom we must hear and whom we must trust and obey in life and in death. (**Barmen Declaration**)

Why did God in His eternal wisdom provide us with the Bible? What is the purpose and the objective of it? It was given to strengthen us, to build us up in our most holy faith. However, our faith cannot be strengthened, we cannot be built up if we do not partake of the food, if we don't go where the food is being served, if we don't take time to eat, remember who we are, and our relationship to God and to Christ. (**Martyn Lloyd-Jones**)

Scripture is meant to enrich our minds, move our hearts and feed our souls. We are to hunger and thirst after the available morsels. We are not to rush past them. (**Robert B. Callahan, Sr.**)

When reading Scripture pause and let it speak to you, let the Holy Spirit work within your mind and reveal the truths contained in the written word. (**Cook Freeman**)

Paul makes it very clear that walking circumspectly, as a wise person, is not happenstance, or the luck of the draw. It requires study, prayer, meditation, consideration and "Above all an intimate knowledge with practical understanding of the Word of God." (**Ruth Paxson**)

(God) is cheated of His glory if we think that the Gospel is given to us either by chance, or by the will or activity of men." (**John Calvin**)

We must always pay attention to this, that the will of God is made known to us in no other manner than by His Word. (**John Calvin**)

When you take away the Gospel or do not apply it, then there is war and enmity between God and man, and between man and man. On the other hand, when you have the proper effect of the Gospel, you give peace and calmness to the conscience, which would otherwise be tormented and disquieted. (**Robert B. Callahan, Sr.**)

It does not expect men to rise up and change it; neither does it simply maintain the status quo. It deals with man himself first, and then, under the influence of this teaching, and with this new understanding, the man himself begins to examine the position and to deal with it. (**Martyn Lloyd-Jones**)

It is a unique book, it is the book, standing apart from all the others. (**Martyn Lloyd-Jones**)

O, what need have we to study the Scriptures, our hearts, and Satan's wiles, that we may not bid this enemy welcome and all the while think it is Christ that is our guest. (**William Gurnall**)

You are in a very difficult world, a sinful world, a world that is dominated by the devil and his cohorts. These principalities and powers! It tells you that you will often find it difficult just to stand on your feet at all. Indeed you will need the whole armor of God; you will need to be "strengthened" with might by his Spirit in the inner man; you will need to be *"strong in the Lord, and in the power of his might."* Then you will be able to stand, but only then. "Quit you like men; be strong! (**Martyn Lloyd-Jones**)

The Bible is full of exhortations, and appeals and arguments and demonstrations and reasonings . . . These New Testament teachings would never have been necessary at all if that other teaching were correct. All the Apostles would have had to say . . . Now then, you have been converted, you have been saved, you have been justified. **(Martyn Lloyd-Jones)**

It (the Word) focuses on God's strengths and our weaknesses. But, in so doing it enables us to grow stronger. The scriptures inform us as to what it means to be a member of Christ's body. When we understand what it is saying to us and how it can help us then, our faith increases, and we become more willing to learn and to obey His commands. **(Robert B. Callahan, Sr.)**

Probably the greatest irony, or incongruity, perpetrated by the church at large in the 20th Century and early 21st Century is that you can have the morality or ethics or, as I prefer, the righteousness of the Bible, without "the whole counsel of God," or the truth as it is revealed in Christ Jesus. You cannot construct a multi-story building without a foundation. There is only one foundation! The truth as it is found in Christ. **(Robert B. Callahan, Sr.)**

Do you really believe that the Bible is the Word of God?" Are you ready to stand for the deity of Christ, for His Virgin birth? For the miracles? Are you ready to stand for the resurrection of Christ as a literal fact? Are you ready to stand for the person of the Holy Spirit?" Are you ready to put on the new man . . . To be filled with the Spirit? To submit yourselves one to another in the fear of Christ? To be strong in the Lord, to put on the whole armor of God? To say with Luther 'Here I stand; I can do no other. **(Martyn Lloyd-Jones)**

The Law and the prophets are not teachings handed on at the pleasure of men or produced by men's minds as their source, but are dictated by the Holy Spirit. **(John Calvin)**

In John's Gospel, the Lord Jesus is called the Word, because first He is the eternal wisdom and will of God, and secondly, because He is the express image of His purpose. **(John Calvin)**

Ministers of the church are ambassadors for testifying and proclaiming the blessing of reconciliation only on the condition that they speak from the gospel as providing a legitimate warrant for what they say. **(John Calvin)**

Our stomachs and bodies are fed by the food we ingest. Some is good for us; some is not. Our hearts, minds, and souls are fed by the teachings we ingest. Some is good; some is not. Therefore, we have to be selective and choose that which is good for us. Our souls are fed by the teaching of the Gospel, when it is efficacious by the power of the Spirit. Therefore, as faith is the life of the soul, all that nourishes and advances faith is compared to food. **(John Calvin)**

It was given to strengthen us, to build us up in our most holy faith. However, our faith cannot be strengthened and we cannot be built up if we do not partake of the food, if we don't go to where the food is being served, if we don't take time to eat, remember who we are, and our relationship to God and to Christ. **(Martyn Lloyd-Jones)**

What is needed is the Spirit opening the Word, and opening my mind and opening my heart. **(Martyn Lloyd-Jones)**

The Holy Spirit is the only true interpreter of the Word. **(William Gurnall)**

A dignitary in the Roman Catholic Church in the Vatican was asked, in private, why their policy regarding opening the scriptures to their members had changed. His reply is worth noting. He said, "I will tell you why we have changed our policy. There is no longer any need for us to be afraid of the scriptures, for this reason, that you Protestants no longer believe in the scriptures. It is you Protestants with your destructive criticism of the Scriptures that have undermined the confidence of the people in the scriptures. So we are able to say that it is we alone who are standing for the scriptures. **(James Millard)**

There is nothing in scripture which may not contribute to your instruction and the training of your life. **(John Calvin)**

The purpose of the doctrine we have been studying, and the knowledge we have been acquiring is one and the same. It is to bring us to the foot of the Cross. It is to bring us to the person of our Lord and Saviour Jesus Christ. It is to bring us into a personal relationship with the Son of God. Everything is directed to kindling a love that cannot be extinguished, one that will grow and grow and grow because it is rooted in an oil providing the necessary nutrients. **(Robert B. Callahan, Sr.)**

With God there (are) no surprises and no emergencies. The Word made flesh was not an afterthought of God. (His) eternal purpose encompasses God's relationship to the saints and faithful, and how they (you and me) are to "become like him and be with him now and forever." **(Ruth Paxson)**

What messages do the epistles present? They are written to the members of the various churches. They all begin by describing our position as members of the community of believers, and then show how in light of this association we are to live.

It is most important for each one to realize these things and by the power of the Holy Spirit to implement and practice them. Think, what an impact this would have on our trials, tests, tribulations, and problems. Think, what an impact it would have on those organizations, we identify as churches if they knew what the writers were really saying and knew how to apply these truths. **(Robert B. Callahan, Sr.)**

Calvin points out that Christ directed his message to the leaders as well as to the people. All of them had contributed to hindering the grace of God as it is to be revealed, or evidenced, in the people.

The evil started with the priests, but the people, due to their own sins, deserved to have corrupt and degraded pastors. Therefore, they all contributed to infecting one another and to turning against God. Woe unto those who do not teach and preach God's Word, who focus on works, but not on the gospel of Christ, and His shed blood. It is as true today as it was then. Nothing has really changed. **(Robert B. Callahan, Sr.)**

The teachings of Christ directly and through the New Testament writers "never contradicts or undoes fundamental biblical teachings with respect to life and living." **(Martyn Lloyd-Jones)**

You find that the Apostle in dealing with the most practical matter suddenly introduces us to the most exalted doctrine. **(Martyn Lloyd-Jones)**

We may be called many, or few, different things, but we must take our stand with this man of God, Paul, and with Scripture. What does the Word teach, what do the Apostles teach? That is what matters, that is what we are called to understand. What we have in Scripture is the only gospel. **(Robert B. Callahan, Sr.)**

God does not communicate to us empty fiction. **(John Calvin)**

When studying Scripture we are not to focus on things, we are to focus on the person of the Lord Jesus Christ. **(Robert B. Callahan, Sr.)**

We must always pay attention to this, that the will of God is made known to us in no other manner than by His Word. **(John Calvin)**

We are not to be unwilling to hear Him (Christ) speaking by the tongue of men. **(John Calvin)**

We are to learn what Scripture offers and to realize that such knowledge is conducive to advancing godliness. **(Robert B. Callahan, Sr.)**

This gospel speaks to those who are called, who live and work in secular environments. The Gospel comes as a contrast:

- It is not an extension of human philosophy;
- It is not an addition to something that men have been able to develop or evolve for themselves;
- The Gospel comes from God; it's His plan, His Good News;
- It comes in the midst of darkness, hopelessness, and despair; and
- It comes purely through the mercy and grace of God.

   (Robert B. Callahan, Sr.)

The Bible starts with the Cross. None of the popular things people like to hear about are possible without the Cross, His death, and His shed blood. (**Robert B. Callahan, Sr.**)

This is not an ordinary truth that the Apostle Paul is describing. He is saying whatever the power of our minds may be, no matter how brilliant we may be, it is not enough, we need the Holy Spirit present and working within us before we can begin to receive and understand God's divine truth. This is hard for some to accept. We are dependent solely and exclusively upon Scripture. There is no saving truth apart from what we find in God's Holy Word. (**Robert B. Callahan, Sr.**)

The Christian teaching realizes that it cannot transform society as a whole; it must go on trusting that gradually the teaching will act as a leaven, and that men will become more and more enlightened. The time lag is not to be explained in terms of the failure of biblical teachings; it is to be explained in terms of the blindness of the world to Christian teaching. Christians have been given wisdom by God and the power to be patient and to wait until the right time for action has arrived. (**Martyn Lloyd-Jones**)

Paul presented the gospel in the following ways:
- He fed them the full doctrine;
- He fed them the details as to how they were to walk;
- He fed them the miracles, teachings, and truths of Christ and Him crucified;
- He did not hesitate, He did not apologize, He proceeded on course;
- He proclaimed the whole gospel, all aspects of it;
- He wanted them to hear it, because he knew if they heard it, that it would change their lives;
- He wanted them to be able to handle the triumphs and defeats of life; and
- He wanted to serve God, and the Lord Jesus Christ, not to please men.

(**Robert B. Callahan, Sr.**)

The Bible is designed to bring us back to God, to humble ourselves before God, and to see our true relationship to Him. **(Robert B. Callahan, Sr.)**

What is true of the Christian?

> He has knowledge of the truth, the *word of truth*, yet knows that it all has come to him through the Word, and that God works through the Word. It all comes from God. **(Robert B. Callahan, Sr.)**

37

WRATH OF GOD

However severe and wrathful a judge God shows Himself to be towards unbelievers (and believers) whenever He punishes them, His primary purpose is to provide counsel for their salvation and to have them come into a right relationship with Himself. This is one way by which He demonstrates His fatherly love. **(John Calvin)**

The wrath of God is the other side of His love. **(Martyn Lloyd-Jones)**

Paul states that we can never understand the love of God until we understand the Doctrine of God's Wrath. Nor can we understand why the Lord Jesus Christ came into the world unless we come to grips with this important doctrine and obtain an understanding of it. **(Robert B. Callahan, Sr.)**

God's wrath consists of the fact that His being is not remote from man but actually interacts with man. His wrath meets man, who is guilty and without excuse. Why? Because, he has received God's proclamation and ignored it. **(Robert B. Callahan, Sr.)**

The teaching regarding love and wrath being incompatible is a denial of God's essence. If we do not consider the Wrath of God against sin, then we cannot fully understand the love of God. Accepting God's wrath against sin enables us to realize the significance of our salvation. **(Robert B. Callahan, Sr.)**

The Wrath of God finally exhibits itself in hell with those who remain outside the life of God. Those who are under the Wrath of God in this life will remain in that condition in the next life. Some people do not like this teaching. They object to it, argue with it, and ignore it. When they do, they are either arguing with Scripture or ignoring it. **(Robert B. Callahan, Sr.)**

God's wrath can only be understood as His real, no compromising, strong NO to sin. Why? Because sin is the rejection of God's love and His purpose for His people. **(Robert B. Callahan, Sr.)**

Jesus Christ is the One who bore the Wrath of God against the sin of the whole human race, and He carried it to the bitter end. **(Robert B. Callahan, Sr.)**

When examining God's wrath it is beneficial to consider it with respect to His grace, which is described as the "timeless kindliness" of God. Grace was not properly understood until the ministry of Jesus Christ. However, His grace does not abrogate the pronouncement of judgment and wrath. **(Robert B. Callahan, Sr.)**

Grace is not a passive attribute of God, which at various times is turned on and goes into motion, and then is turned off. It is a reality! God's grace (unmerited and unconditional favor) is bestowed continuously. Therefore, His wrath is greatly mitigated by His grief and mercy toward those who are *in Christ*. **(Robert B. Callahan, Sr.)**

Though dead in our trespasses and sins, and under the Wrath of God, helpless and hopeless, what happened?

God, whom we disobeyed, offended, and against whom we sinned, provided a way for us to be reconciled to Himself.

> He sent His own Son to be the Atonement for our sins. He sent Him to Calvary's Hill with all the accompanying suffering, shame, and cruelty.
>
> God offers us complete deliverance and reconciliation *despite* the fact we deserve only His wrath.
>
> That is the Love of God! **(Robert B. Callahan, Sr.)**

He removes unfruitful branches, so they can be thrown into the fire and burned. He gets rid of them. (**John Calvin**)

The righteousness of God is revealed from faith to faith, from the faith of one believer to the faith of another, but the wrath of God is revealed from heaven. The Holy Spirit has bestowed upon preachers and teachers the ability to tell people of God's grace, to proclaim the Gospel, and to communicate the faith, but the wrath is from heaven, therefore, it is to be proclaimed by preachers and teachers. When considering God's Word, bear in mind, it is a privilege to announce faith and righteousness, but it is a duty to announce wrath and unrighteousness. (**Robert B. Callahan, Sr.**)

www.ingramcontent.com/pod-product-compliance
Lightning Source LLC
Chambersburg PA
CBHW062027220426
43662CB00010B/1509